PSYCHOLOGY RESEARCH PROGRESS

ADDICTION TO EXERCISE

A SYMPTOM OR A DISORDER?

PSYCHOLOGY RESEARCH PROGRESS

Additional books in this series can be found on Nova's website at:

https://www.novapublishers.com/catalog/index.php?cPath=23_29&seriesp=
Psychology+Research+Progress

Additional e-books in this series can be found on Nova's website at:

https://www.novapublishers.com/catalog/index.php?cPath=23_29&seriespe=
Psychology+Research+Progress

ADDICTION TO EXERCISE

A SYMPTOM OR A DISORDER?

ATTILA SZABO

Nova Science Publishers, Inc.
New York

LIBRARY OF CONGRESS CATALOGING-IN-PUBLICATION DATA

Szabo, Attila, 1950-
 Addiction to exercise : a symptom or a disorder? / Attila Szabo.
   p. ; cm.
 Includes bibliographical references and index.
 ISBN 978-1-60876-789-2 (softcover)
 1. Exercise addiction. I. Title.
 [DNLM: 1. Behavior, Addictive. 2. Exercise--psychology. WM 176 S996a 2009]
 RC569.5.E94S93 2009
 616.85'84--dc22
                                                                    2009048898

Published by Nova Science Publishers, Inc. ✤ New York

CONTENTS

PREFACE

This book evaluates the psychological concept of exercise addiction from a scholastically multidisciplinary perspective. The most recent developments in the area of investigation are evaluated with reference to theory and critical analysis of extant research. The book summarizes the current knowledge about the psycho-physiological nature of exercise addiction. Further, it presents the conceptual hegemony in addressing the problem of exercise addiction within the scientific community. The characteristic and most prevalent symptoms of the disorder are discussed alongside the modes of risk-assessment. Subsequently, the underlying motives and several theoretical models of exercise addiction are reviewed. Finally, the research on exercise addiction is evaluated and directions for future research are suggested. Difference is made between primary exercise addiction in which the exercise behavior is the problem and secondary exercise addiction in which exercise is used as a means in achieving another objective, like weight loss. This book concludes with two brief sections summarizing plainly what we know today and what we still need to know about exercise addiction.

ABOUT THE AUTHOR

 Dr Attila Szabo has completed his university education in Montreal, Canada. In 1986 he has obtained a BSc in Psychology from Concordia University and three years later he has completed the MSc studies in Biology at the same university. In 1993 he got a PhD degree from the University of Montreal in the area of Human Movement Studies. In 1997 he was appointed as a Senior Lecturer in Sports Sciences at Nottingham Trent University in the United Kingdom. Four years later, he was promoted to Reader in Sport and Exercise Psychology in the School of Biomedical and Natural Sciences where he worked until July 2005. Subsequently, he has moved to Hungary. Currently, he is Deputy Director and Associate Professor in the Institute of Health Promotion and Sports Sciences at the Eötvös Loránd University in Budapest. Here, in 2009 based on research and teaching accomplishment records and internationally recognized contribution to field of exercise addiction, Dr Szabo has obtained the scientific rank and title of Habilitated Doctor (Dr Habil) in Psychology. Apart from his University affiliation, Dr Szabo leads the research at the National Institute for Sport Talent Care and Sports Services in Budapest, where his main work comprises the psychological testing of young elite athletes, the future Hungarian Olympic hopes. The author is member of several national and international scholastic organizations. He has over 150 scientific publications and conference presentations. Dr Szabo is the academic who has introduced scholastic research on the internet - in 1996 - not only by writing and publishing the first set of guidelines for internet research in peer reviewed journals, but also by publishing reports based on data gathered from the internet.

PEER REVIEWED PUBLISHED WORKS FROM THE AUTHOR ON WHICH THIS MONOGRAPH IS BASED

Szabo, A. (1995). The impact of exercise deprivation on well-being of habitual exercisers. *The Australian Journal of Science and Medicine in Sport, 27*, 68-75.

Szabo, A., Frenkl, R., and Caputo, A. (1996). Deprivation feelings, anxiety, and commitment to various forms of physical activity: A cross-sectional study on the Internet. *Psychologia, 39*, 223-230.

Szabo, A., Frenkl, R., and Caputo, A. (1997). Relationships between addiction to running, commitment to running, and deprivation from running. *European Yearbook of Sport Psychology, 1*, 130-147.

Szabo, A. (1998). Studying the psychological impact of exercise deprivation: are experimental studies hopeless? *Journal of Sport Behavior*, 21, 139-147.

Szabo, A. (2000). Physical activity and psychological dysfunction. In Biddle, S., Fox, K., and Boutcher, S. (Eds.). *Physical Activity and Psychological Well-Being* (Chapter 7, pp. 130-153). Routledge, London

Szabo, A. (2001). *The dark side of sports and exercise: Research Dilemmas*. Paper presented at the 10th World Congress of Sport Psychology, May 30, 2001, Skiathos, Greece.

Terry, A., Szabo, A., and Griffiths, M. D. (2004). The exercise addiction inventory: A new brief screening tool. *Addiction Research and Theory, 12*, 489–499.

Griffiths, M.D., Szabo, A., and Terry, A. (2005). The exercise addiction inventory: a quick and easy screening tool for health practitioners. *British Journal of Sports Medicine, 39, e30* (http://bjsportmed.com/cgi/content/full/39/6/e30)

Szabo, A., Ainsworth, S.E., and Danks, P.K. (2005). Experimental comparison of the psychological benefits of aerobic exercise, humor, and music. *HUMOR: International Journal of Humor Research, 18(3),* 235-246.

Szabo, A. (2006). Comparison of the psychological effects of exercise and humor. In Andrew M. Lane (Ed.). *Mood and Human Performance: Conceptual, Measurement, and Applied Issues (Chapter 10, pp.201-216).* Hauppauge, NY: Nova Science Publishers, Inc.

Rendi, M., Szabo, A., and Szabó, T. (2007). Exercise and Internet addiction: commonalities and differences between two problematic behaviors. *International Journal of Mental Health and Addiction. 5,* 219-232.

Szabo, A., and Griffiths, M.D. (2007). Exercise addiction in British sport science students. *International Journal of Mental Health and Addiction, 5(1),* 25-28.

Szabo, A., Velenczei, A., Szabó, T., and Kovács, A. (2007). Exercise addiction. *Magyar Sporttudományi Szemle (Hungarian Review of Sport Sciences), 8(31),* 43(Abs.).

Chapter 1

INTRODUCTION

1.0 – FROM HEALTHY TO UNHEALTHY EXERCISE

1.1. Exercise is a Good Thing (in Moderation)

As consequence of technological development, machines are taking over man's work, which increases the likelihood of sedentary lifestyle in the contemporary societies. In most developed nations the amount of physical activity involved in the daily survival activities has been reduced to a minimum. However, the human body evolved to face and deal with physical challenges such as hunting, hiding, building shelters, and so on (Jones and Weinhouse, 1979; Péronnet and Szabo, 1993). Since the technological revolution takes place at an extremely fast pace in contrast to the biological evolution, the human organism cannot adapt evolutionarily to this very rapid shift from a physically active to physically passive or sedentary lifestyle. Therefore, it is unlikely that it can preserve its healthy or "natural" state of equilibrium, also known as homeostasis, in lack of physical challenges (Péronnet and Szabo, 1993). The only conceivable remedy for compensating for the lost physical activity that were part of humans' survival activities is to become increasingly more active in leisure activities. Indeed, in many industrialized nations substantial effort is invested in promoting physical activity, which is associated with healthy, positive, or even 'politically correct' forms of behaviors (Edwards, 2007). The mental and physiological benefits of physical activity are almost undisputed. There is a strong consensus within the scientific circles with regard to the value of integrating physical activity in one's regular lifestyle (Bouchard, Shephard, and Stephens, 1994; Warburton, Nicol, and Bredin, 2006).

According to the most recently published guidelines of the American Colleges of Sports Medicine (ACSM) and the American Heart Association, to promote and maintain health, healthy adults aged 18 to 65 years should engage in moderate-intensity aerobic or endurance exercises at least five times a week for at least 30 minutes on each occasion or high-intensity aerobic exercises three times a week for a minimum of 20 minutes each time (Haskell et al., 2007). Nevertheless, a combination of moderate- and high-intensity physical activities could also be adopted to meet the recommendations. For example, an individual can meet the recommendation by jogging or running 20 minutes twice a week and then walking briskly or cycling at a leisure rhythm for 30 minutes on two other days on the same week. Moderate-intensity aerobic exercise that is generally equivalent to a brisk walk, and noticeably increases the heart rate, could be accumulated to achieve the 30-minute minimum by performing separate bouts each lasting 10 to 15 minutes (Haskell et al., 2007). High-intensity exercises are represented by physical activities like jogging or running (depending on the person's physical condition), fast swimming, speed skating, or effortful cycling and to qualify as such they should cause rapid breathing and a substantial increase in heart rate. In addition to aerobic activities, every individual should perform physical exercises that maintain or increase muscular strength and resistance a minimum of twice every week. Finally, Haskell et al. state that since there is a dose-response relationship between physical activity and health, individuals may be better off exceeding the minimum recommended amounts of physical activity to further augment fitness, maintain or reduce weight, and to reduce the risk of various diseases.

Such a recommendation clearly mirrors to justifiability of large doses of physical activity. Nevertheless, Haskell et al. warn that increasing the dose of physical activity beyond the recommendations of the ACSM also increases the risks for injury and even cardiac complications. In spite of such warning, the positive correlation between the amount of exercise and health may be misinterpreted and in isolated cases (the term to remember throughout this monograph is: *isolated case* or *very rare case*) physical activity may be abused to lead to undesirable or harmful physical and psychological states. Indeed overdoing an adopted physical activity may not only result in severe physical injuries, but also in irreversible health effects or even fatal consequence (Cumella, 2005).

Overexercising to the point where one loses control over her or his exercise routine and walks a "path of self-destruction" (Morgan, 1979) is referred to as *exercise addiction* (Griffiths, 1997; Thaxton, 1982). The same concept is also often described as *exercise dependence* by a number of scholars (Cockerill and

Riddington, 1996; Hausenblas and Symons Downs, 2002a). Further, some academics refer to the condition as *obligatory exercising* (Pasman and Thompson, 1988). In the public or mass media the condition is most frequently termed as *compulsive exercise* (Eberle, 2004) or as *exercise abuse* (Davis, 2000). It is important to note that all these synonymous words describe the same psychological condition. However, in light of some credible arguments, as elaborated below, alternating the terminology may be unproductive.

Whilst the term "dependence" is used as a synonym for addiction, the latter includes the former and also includes "compulsion" (Goodman, 1990). Accordingly, a general formula for addiction may be: *addiction = dependence + compulsion*. Goodman specifies that not all dependencies and compulsions may be classified as an addiction. Therefore, in this book the term *exercise addiction* is considered to be the most appropriate because it incorporates both, dependence and compulsion. The rest of the text will explore this rare but intensively researched psychological condition.

1.2. From Commitment to Addiction

Glasser (1976) believed that too much of a good thing is better than too much of a bad thing. Therefore, he has introduced the term *positive addiction* in the scientific literature to describe the personally and socially beneficial aspects of a regular and persistent exercise behavior in contrast to some self-destructive behaviors like tobacco, drug, or alcohol abuse. The "positive" prefix in conjunction with the term addiction led to the widespread and careless use of the term *exercise addiction* within both athletic and scientific populations. Indeed, a number of runners have claimed that they were *addicted* to running while they only referred to their high level of commitment and dedication to their chosen exercise. Morgan (1979) long ago has acknowledged that this is a semantic problem, because the "positive" prefix deters attention from incidences where a transition occurs from high levels of commitment to exercise to addiction to exercise. Therefore, to discuss the negative aspects of exaggerated exercise behavior, he has introduced the term *negative addiction* as an antonym to Glasser's positive addiction. The fact is, however, that all addictions represent a dysfunction and, therefore, they are *always* negative (Rozin and Stoess, 1993).

In fact, Glasser's (1976) "positive" notion referred to the benefits of *commitment* to physical exercise (a healthy behavior) in contrast to the negative effects of "unhealthy" addictions. Positive addiction in sport science and psychology literature may be perceived as a synonym for *commitment to exercise*

(Carmack and Martens, 1979; Pierce, 1994). However, when commitment to exercise is used as a synonym to *exercise addiction* or to *exercise dependence* as termed by some scholars (Conboy, 1994; Sachs, 1981; Thornton and Scott, 1995) a major conceptual error is emerging. For example, Thornton and Scott (1995) reported that they could classify 77% of a small sample (n = 40) of runners as moderately or highly addicted to running. Such a figure is enormous if one thinks that among twenty thousand runners in a marathon race, for example, more than three quarters of the participants may be addicted! The figure is obviously exaggerated (Szabo, 2000). Therefore, some scholars have realized this problem and have attempted to draw a line between commitment and addiction to exercise (Chapman and De Castro, 1990; Summers and Hinton, 1986; Szabo, 2000; Szabo, Frenkl, and Caputo, 1997).

Commitment to exercise is a measure of how devoted an individual is to her/his activity. It is a measure of the strength of adherence to an adopted, healthy or beneficial activity that is a part of the daily life of the individual. For committed people, satisfaction, enjoyment, and achievement derived from their activity are the incentives that motivate them to stick to their sport or exercise (Chapman and De Castro, 1990). Sachs (1981) believed that commitment to exercise results from the intellectual analysis of the rewards, including social relationships, health, status, prestige, or even monetary advantages, gained from the activity. Committed exercisers, according to Sachs: 1) exercise for extrinsic rewards, 2) view their exercise as an important, but not the central part of their lives, and 3) may not experience major withdrawal symptoms when they cannot exercise for some reason (Summers and Hinton, 1986). Probably the key point is that committed exercisers *control* their activity (Johnson, 1995) rather than being controlled by the activity. In contrast to committed exercisers, addicted exercisers are: 1) more likely to exercises for intrinsic rewards, 2) aware that exercise is the central part of their lives and 3) experiencing severe deprivation feelings when they are prevented to exercise (Sachs, 1981; Summers and Hinton, 1986).

Chapter 2

DEFINITION

2.0 - THE CONCEPT OF EXERCISE ADDICTION

2.1. Definition of Exercise Addiction

Before attempting to define exercise addiction, it should be noted that there is no simple or standard definition for addiction (Johnson, 1994). In Goodman's (1990) view, addiction is a behavioral process that could provide either pleasure or relief from internal discomfort (stress, anxiety, etc.) and it is characterized by repeated failure to control the behavior (state of powerlessness) and maintenance of the behavior in spite of major negative consequences. From Sachs' criteria mentioned in the previous section it is clear that exercise addiction includes: 1) salience, and 2) withdrawal symptoms. Salience, or high priority in life, and preoccupation with exercise, accompanied by increased bouts of exercise, are inherent in the term overexercising. The presence of withdrawal symptoms, on the other hand, is a separate manifestation of the problem.

It appears that the presence of withdrawal symptoms is a key feature in the description and definition of exercise addiction. Indeed, long ago Sachs and Pargman (1979) defined the exercise addicts as *"persons who demonstrate psychological and/or physiological dependence upon a regularly experienced regimen of running. In these individuals the unfulfilled need or desire to run produces withdrawal symptoms"* (p. 145). Later Sachs (1981) defined exercise addiction in reference to runners as *"addiction of a psychological and/or physiological nature, upon a regular regimen of running, characterized by withdrawal symptoms after 24 to 36 hours without participation"* (p. 118). Similarly, Morgan (1979) thought that exercise addiction is only present when

"...*two requirements are met. First, the individual must require daily exercise in order to exist or cope: the runner cannot live without running. Second, if deprived of exercise the individual must manifest various withdrawal symptoms (e.g. depression, anxiety, or irritability* (p. 5). Others echo these definitions in the literature (Furst and Germone, 1993; Morris, 1989; Sachs and Pargman, 1984) and strengthen the assumption that withdrawal symptoms are a key aspect of exercise addiction. But could the mere experience of withdrawal symptoms imply or suggest the presence of exercise addiction in a diagnostic way? To answer this question a closer inspection of the literature examining withdrawal symptoms in habitual exercisers is necessary.

2.2. WITHDRAWAL SYMPTOMS

The literature reveals that withdrawal symptoms, although marking, are only one of the several symptoms of exercise addiction (Brown, 1993; Griffiths, 1997). Incorrectly, in the past, many studies have simply assessed the mere presence, rather than the type, frequency, and the intensity of withdrawal symptoms (Szabo, 1995; Szabo et al., 1997). However, most habitual exercisers report negative psychological symptoms for times when they are prevented from exercise for an unexpected reason (Szabo, Frenkl, and Caputo, 1996; Szabo et al., 1997). Indeed, Szabo et al. (1996) conducted a survey research on the Internet and have shown that even participants in physically "light effort" types of exercises, like bowling, reported withdrawal symptoms when the activity (in this case bowling) was prevented. However, the intensity or severity of the withdrawal symptoms reported by the bowlers was less than that of aerobic dancers, weight-trainers, cross-trainers, and fencers (Szabo et al., 1996).

Consequently, it must be appreciated that the presence of withdrawal symptoms alone is insufficient for diagnosing exercise addiction. The intensity of these symptoms is a crucial factor in separating committed from addicted exercisers. Cockerill and Riddington (1996) do not even mention withdrawal symptoms in their list of symptoms associated with exercise addiction. In fact the presence of withdrawal symptoms, in many forms of physical activity, suggests that exercise has a positive effect on people's psychological and physical health. This positive effect is then, obviously, missed when an interruption in the habitual activity is necessary for an unwanted reason.

It is clear then symptom-based diagnosis of exercise addiction cannot be made simply on the presence or absence of withdrawal symptoms. The inspection of other symptoms, such as salience and tolerance that are common to other forms of substance (e.g. alcohol) as well as behavioral addictions (e.g. gambling), and their co-occurrence needs to be evaluated. Indeed, most questionnaires aimed at the screening of exercise addiction are symptom-based. Six common symptoms of behavioral addiction were identified through the systematic observation of several behaviors such as exercise, sex, gambling, video games, and also the Internet. Based on Brown's (1993) general components of addictions, Griffiths (1996, 1997, and 2002) has reiterated them into six common components of addiction. Later, Griffiths (2005) proposed a "components" model for addiction, going beyond exercise addiction whilst bringing the latter under a common umbrella with other addictions, based on six most common symptoms (salience, mood modification, tolerance, withdrawal, conflict and relapse). Griffiths suggests that addictions are a part of a biopsychosocial process and evidence is growing that most if not all addictive behaviors seem to share these commonalities.

Chapter 3

SYMPTOMS

3.0 – COMMON SYMPTOMS OF EXERCISE ADDICTION

3.1. Six Common Symptoms in Griffiths' (2005) "Components" Model

3.1.1. Salience –

This symptom is present when the physical activity or exercises becomes the most important activity in the persons' life and dominates their thinking (preoccupation and cognitive distortions), feelings (cravings) and behavior (deterioration of social behaviors). For instance, even if the persons are not actually engaged in exercise they will be thinking about the next time they will be. The mind of the addicted individual wanders off to exercise during other daily activities like driving, having meals, attending meetings, and even between conversations with friends. The closer is the planned time for exercise the greater is the urge and even anxiety or fear from not starting on time. The addicted exerciser is literally obsessed with exercise and regardless of the time of the day, place, or activity performed her or his mind is directed towards exercise during the majority of waking hours.

3.1.2. Mood Modification –

This symptom refers to the subjective experiences that people report as a consequence of engaging in the particular activity and could be seen as a coping strategy (i.e., they experience an arousing "buzz" or a "high", or paradoxically tranquillizing feel of "escape" or "numbing"). Most exercisers report a positive feeling state and pleasant exhaustion after a session of exercise. However, the person addicted to exercise would seek mood modification not necessarily for the gain or the positive mental effect of exercise, but rather for the modification or avoidance of the negative psychological feeling states that she or he would experience if the exercise session were missed.

3.1.3. Tolerance –

It is the process whereby increasing amounts of the particular activity are required to achieve the former effects. For instance, a gambler may have to gradually increase the size of the bet to experience the euphoric or satisfying effect that was initially obtained by a much smaller bet. The runner needs to run longer distances to experience the runner's high[1] (Stoll, 1997), a euphoric feeling state described later. Similarly, the addicted exerciser needs larger and larger doses of exercise to derive the effects experienced previously with lower amounts of exercise. Tolerance is the main reason why individuals addicted to exercise progressively and continuously increase the frequency, duration, and possibly intensity of their workouts.

3.1.4. Withdrawal Symptoms –

These symptoms are the unpleasant psychological and physical feeling states, which occur when exercise is discontinued or it is significantly reduced. The most commonly reported symptoms are guilt, irritability, anxiety, sluggishness, feeling fat, lacking energy, and being in bad mood or depressed. The intensity of these states is severe in people affected by exercise addiction to the extent that they really feel miserable when the need of exercise is not fulfilled. The manifestation of these withdrawal symptoms in addicted individuals is clearly different from those experienced by committed exercisers who simply feel a void, or that something is missing, when exercising is not possible for a reason. Addicted exercisers have to exercise to avoid withdrawal symptoms even at the expense of other more important life obligations. In contrast, committed exercisers look forward to the next opportunity while prioritizing their obligations (Szabo, 1995).

3.1.5. Conflict –

This symptom represents the conflict between the exercise addicts and others around them (interpersonal conflict), conflict with other daily activities (job, social life, hobbies and interests) or from within the individual themselves (intra-

---

1 A pleasant feeling associated with positive self image, sense of vitality, control, and a sense of fulfilment reported by runners as well as by other exercisers after a certain amount and intensity of exercise. The feeling has been associated with increased levels of endogenous opioids and catecholamines observed after exercise.

psychic conflict) which are concerned with the particular activity. Interpersonal conflict usually results from neglect of the relationship with friends or family because of the exaggerated time devoted to exercise. Conflict in daily activities arises because of the abnormally high priority given to exercise in contrast to some basic survival activities like cleaning, taking care of bills, working, or studying for exams. Intra-psychic conflict occurs when the addicted person has realized that fulfilling the need to exercise takes a toll on other life endeavors, but she or he is unable to cut down or to control the exercise behavior.

3.1.6. Relapse –

This is the tendency for repeated reversions to earlier patterns of exercise after a break whether that is voluntary or involuntary. The phenomenon is similar to that observed in alcoholics who stop drinking for a period of time and then start over again and drink as much – if not more – than prior to the break from drinking. Relapse could be observed after injury (which is involuntary) or after a planned reduction in exercise volume as a consequence of personal decision to put a halt on the unhealthy pattern of exercise behavior or as a consequence of professional advice. Upon resumption of the activity, addicted individuals could soon end up exercising as much or even more as before the reduction of their volume of exercise.

3.2. OTHER SYMPTOMS OBSERVED IN EXERCISE ADDICTION

3.2.1. Loss of Control over Life-Activities (Griffiths, 1997) –

The internal drive or urge for exercise becomes psychologically so intense that it preoccupies attention in the majority of waking hours by dominating the person's thoughts. Consequently, the affected individual is unable to pay attention or to properly concentrate on other daily activities. Until that urge is satisfied, other life-activities are deficiently performed or totally neglected. Upon fulfillment of the need to exercise, the affected person may function well and take care of some other mundane obligations but such a "normal" functioning is limited to the period encompassing the acute effects of the previous session of exercise or until the urge for another bout of exercise starts to rise again.

3.2.2. Loss of Control over One's Exercise Behavior (Cockerill and Riddington, 1996; Johnson, 1995) –

This is a phenomenon where self-set resolutions cannot be kept. The exerciser simply cannot resist the urge to exercise. While she or he may try to set limits in her/his exercise patterns, she/he is unable to respect those self-set limits. In short, lack of control denotes the inability to exercise with moderation. This is a phenomenon also observable in alcoholics (and in most addictions in general) who after several incidences of heavy drinking, and some severe consequences of such drinking pattern, make the resolution not to get drunk again. However, on the same day later, after making such a resolution, they get drunk again.

3.2.3. Negative, Non-Injury Related, Life Consequences (Griffiths, 1997) –

Negative life events may occur as a result of overexercising. If life activities are ignored or superficially performed as a result of excessive exercise and too much preoccupation with exercise, on the long term, negative life consequences may emerge involving even loss of employment, poor academic performance, break-up in relationships and friendships, and other consequences generally considered to have undesirable effects on the person's life.

3.2.4. Risk of Self-Injury (De Coverley Veale, 1987; Wichmann and Martin, 1992) –

At times of mild injuries the addicted exerciser cannot abstain from exercise and, thus, assumes the risk of self-injury by maintaining her/his physical activity. In more severe cases, the affected individual needs to see a medical professional who may advice the person to refrain from exercising until full recovery takes place. In spite of medical advice, the person addicted to exercise, will likely resume her or his exercise immediately upon experiencing minor alleviation in the discomfort associated with the injury – or in the early stages of recovery – thus exposing her- / himself to further and possibly more severe injuries, triggering often irreversible health damages.

3.2.5. Social Selection and Withdrawal (Cockerill And Riddington, 1996) –

This is a behavior tendency by which the addicted person identifies with others who approve her or his exercise behavior and avoids the company of those who criticize her/his physical activity pattern. Such a social gravitation is generally observable in individuals suffering from others forms of behavioral (e.g. gambling) or substance (e.g. alcohol) addictions.

3.2.6. Lack of Compromise (Wichmann and Martin, 1992) –

This symptom is closely related to the loss of control described above. Although there may be several warning signs related to the neglect of family or work responsibilities because of excessive exercise, the signs are insufficient to trigger a decision to compromise. Consequently, other life-commitments remain ignored even though the affected person is aware that the end result may be worse than undesirable.

3.2.7. Denial of a Problem or Self-Justification (Wichmann and Martin, 1992) –

This represents a psychological defense mechanism known as rationalization. The person addicted to exercise explains or justifies the problem via conscious search for reasons why exercise, even in massive volume, is beneficial. The mass media and even scientific reports provide abundant reasons that could be used in the rationalization. The ACSM guidelines for exercise and the positive correlation between the dose of exercise and health (Haskell et al., 2007) are excellent anchors for justifying the exaggerated amounts of exercise.

3.2.8. Full Awareness of the Problem (De Coverley Veale, 1987) –

The exercise addict may know well that there are problems with her/his exercise behavior through feedback from other people or from some negative life-events directly resulting from overexercising. However, she/he feels powerless to take action against the problem.

3.3. A NEWER CLASSIFICATION FOR BEHAVIORAL ADDICTIONS IN GENERAL

More recently, two German scientists, Grüsser and Thalemann (2006) presented a newer classification for behavioral addictions based on some relatively common characteristics noticeable in several forms of addictions. These scholars conjecture that these characteristic symptoms may be signs for the possible diagnosis of a behavioral addiction, thus including exercise addiction. Nevertheless, the authors emphasize that cases need to be examined individually to determine whether the heavy involvement with the given behavior is indeed addictive or just an excessive one (non-pathological or related to another dysfunction). Indeed, symptoms alone may not be sufficient for the correct diagnosis, but a collection of *severe typical symptoms* in conjunction with *history of negative consequences,* due to the excessive indulgence in a given behavior, may pinpoint the presence of addiction. Grüsser's and Thalemann's characteristics are:

1. The behavior is exhibited over a long period of at least 12 months in an excessive, aberrant form, deviating from the norm in frequency and intensity
2. Loss of control over the excessive behavior (duration, frequency, intensity, risk) when the behavior started
3. Reward effect (e.g. excessive exercises is considered to be rewarding)
4. Development of tolerance (the behavior is conducted longer, more often and more intensively in order to achieve the desired effect; in unvaried form, intensity and frequency the desired effect fails to appear)
5. The behavior that was initially perceived as pleasant, positive and rewarding is increasingly considered to be unpleasant in the course of the addiction
6. Irresistible urge/craving to execute the behavior
7. Function (the behavior is chiefly performed to regulate emotions/mood)
8. Expectancy of effect (pleasant feelings are anticipated to result from the behavior)
9. Limited pattern of behavior (does not wish to try out new things)
10. Cognitive occupation with the build-up, execution and follow-up activities of the excessive behavior and possibly the anticipated effects of the excessively executed behavior
11. Irrational, perception of different aspects of the excessive behavior

12. Withdrawal symptoms (psychological and physical)
13. Continued execution of the excessive behavior despite negative consequences (health-related, occupational, social)
14. Conditioned/learned reactions (resulting from the confrontation with internal and external stimuli associated with the excessive behavior as well as from cognitive occupation with the excessive behavior)
15. Suffering (desire to alleviate perceived suffering)

Grüsser's and Thalemann's (2006) list of characteristics is clearly longer than the symptoms contained within the "components" model of addiction (Griffiths, 2005). However, the list incorporates most if not all, directly or implicitly, six components of addiction proposed by Griffiths. The question is whether fewer but typical symptoms of addiction are sufficient to help health professionals in the identification of the disorder or whether a longer list is needed? Albrecht, Kirschner, and Grüsser (2007) believe that clinical orientations, also reinforced by scientific evidence, highlight the commonalities between substance-related and non-substance related behavioral addictions. They believe that a standardized classification should describe all excessive or abused behaviors that meet the criteria of addictions as an addiction disorder and incorporate them into the diagnostic criteria. These criteria would facilitate the accurate diagnosis (by using valid and reliable instruments) and also aid in the effective treatment of affected individuals. It is clear then that the proper assessment of exercise addiction is crucial in the identification the addiction as a dysfunction.

Chapter 4

ASSESSMENT

4.0. ASSESSMENT OF EXERCISE ADDICTION

Although symptoms are critical in the assessment of a health condition, as seen in the previous section, exercise addiction cannot be positively assessed simply on the basis of the presence or absence of withdrawal symptoms. A combination of symptoms co-occurring is a more precise index of maladaptive exercise. Currently, there are several exercise addiction questionnaires that are based on the most common symptoms of addictions. In general, the frequency and intensity of the symptoms reported by the respondents is computed to yield an exercise addiction score. However, these scores only measure the *degree of* or *the susceptibility to* exercise addiction, rather than positively diagnose the condition. In the following section the psychometrically validated most popular tools used for assessing exercise addiction will be briefly presented and evaluated.

4.1. THE EXERCISE ADDICTION INVENTORY, (EAI - TERRY, SZABO, AND GRIFFITHS, 2004)

This is the shortest psychometrically validated questionnaire to date (Appendix A). It consists of only six statements that correspond to the "components" model of addiction (Griffiths, 2005). Each statement is rated on a five-point Likert scale. The statements are coded so that the high scores reflect attributes of addictive exercise behavior: 1="strongly disagree", 2="disagree", 3="neither agree nor disagree", 4="agree", 5="strongly agree". The six statements that make up the inventory are: 1) *"Exercise is the most important thing in my life*" (salience), 2) "*Conflicts have arisen between me and my family and/or my partner about the amount of exercise I do*" (conflict), 3) "*I use exercise as a way of changing my mood*" (mood modification), 4) "*Over time I have increased the amount of exercise I do in a day*" (tolerance), 5) "*If I have to miss an exercise session I feel moody and irritable*" (withdrawal symptoms), and 6) "*If I cut down the amount of exercise I do, and then start again, I always end up exercising as often as I did before*" (relapse).

The EAI cut-off score for individuals considered at-risk of exercise addiction is 24. This cut off represents those individuals with scores in the top 15% of the total scale score. High scores were considered to be the most problematic for the individual. A score of 13 to 23 was chosen to be indicative of a potentially symptomatic person and a score of 0 to 12 was deemed to indicate an asymptomatic individual. The EAI was developed on the basis of a sample of 200 habitual exercisers. The internal reliability of the original scale was excellent (α = .84) and its concurrent validity was at least r = .80.

The EAI is the most recent and the shortest tool aimed at the assessment of risk of exercise addiction. It is also the easiest to interpret and the fastest to administer. The authors developed the scale to aid non-psychologist medical personnel, like orthopedic specialists (who often encounter individuals addicted to exercise in their practice due to injury) to easily and quickly gauge whether the person may be at risk of exercise addiction.

4.2. THE OBLIGATORY EXERCISE QUESTIONNAIRE (OEQ - PASMAN AND THOMPSON, 1988)

This questionnaire was a pioneering instrument aimed at the assessment of exercise addiction. It was modified from the Obligatory Running Questionnaire (ORQ - Blumenthal, O'Toole, and Chang, 1984). Later the OEQ has been modified to a version that is a more general measure of exercise activity (Thompson and Pasman, 1991). The new version of the questionnaire consists of 20 items pertaining to exercises habits, which are rated on a 4-point frequency scale: 1-never, 2-sometimes, 3-usually, 4-always. Two of the items are inversely rated during scoring. The psychometric properties of the questionnaire have been well established (Coen and Ogles, 1993). The internal reliability of the OEQ was reported to be α =. 96 and its concurrent validity was r = .96 (Thompson and Pasman, 1991).

Ackard, Brehm, and Steffen (2002) found that the OEQ (1991 version) has three subscales. These are exercise fixation (items associated with missed exercise and exercise to compensate for perceived overeating), exercise frequency (addressing frequency and type of exercise) and exercise commitment (indicating a sense of routine which cannot be missed). Ackard et al. believe that these subscales highlight the multifaceted nature of excessive exercise.

4.3. THE EXERCISE DEPENDENCE QUESTIONNAIRE (EDQ - OGDEN, VEALE, AND SUMMERS, 1997)

The EDQ was developed with a sample of 449 participants who exercised for more than 4 hours a week. The EDQ consists of 29 items and it has 8 subscales: 1) interference with social/family/work life, 2) positive reward, 3) withdrawal symptoms, 4) exercise for weight control, 5) insight into problem, 6) exercise for social reasons, 7) exercise for health reasons, and 8) stereotyped behavior. The EDQ was found to have moderate to good internal reliability ranging from $\alpha =. 52$ to $\alpha =. 84$. Its concurrent validity with other instruments has not been reported. Further, certain items assess attitudes and social practices rather than addiction. Consequently, the EDQ has been used only on relatively few occasions in researching exercise addiction.

4.4. EXERCISE DEPENDENCE SCALE (EDS - HAUSENBLAS AND SYMONS DOWNS, 2002B)

Hausenblas and Symons Downs (2002a; 2002b) have developed the Exercise Dependence Scale (EDS). Exercise is described as a craving for exercise that results in uncontrollable excessive physical activity and manifests in physiological symptoms, psychological symptoms, or both (Hausenblas and Symons Downs, 2002a). The Exercise Dependence Scale is based on the Diagnostic and Statistical Manual of Mental Disorder-IV criteria for substance dependence (DSM IV - American Psychiatric Association, 1994). The Exercise Dependence Scale is able to differentiate between at-risk, non-dependent-symptomatic, and nondependent-asymptomatic individuals. It can also specify whether individuals may have a physiological dependence (evidence of withdrawal) or no physiological dependence (no evidence of withdrawal).

On the EDS 21-items are rated on a 6-point Likert frequency scale ranging from 1 (never) to 6 (always). Evaluation is made in reference to the DSM-IV criteria (APA, 1994), screening for the presence of three or more of the following symptoms, most of them described in the previous section: 1) tolerance, 2) withdrawal, 3) intention effects (exercise is often taken in larger amounts or over longer period than was intended), 4) loss of control, 5) time (a great deal of time is spent in activities conducive to the obtainment of exercise), 6) conflict, and 7) continuance (exercise is continued despite knowledge of persistent or recurrent physical or psychological problems that are likely to have been caused or exacerbated by exercise).

A total score and subscale scores can be calculated for the EDI. The higher the score, the higher is the risk for addiction. The scale is rated with the aid of a scoring manual that comprises flowchart-format decision rules. The rules specify the items or the combinations of the items that that help in classifying the individual as being at risk, non-addicted-symptomatic or non-addicted asymptomatic on each criterion. Individuals who score in the addiction range, defined as 4 - 5 (out of 6) on the Likert scale on at least three of the seven criteria, are classified as 'at risk' for exercise addiction. Those who fulfil at least three criteria in the non-addicted symptomatic range, scoring around 3 on the Likert scale, or a combination of at least three criteria in the 'at risk' and non-addicted symptomatic range, but did not meet the criteria for exercise addiction, are classified as non-addicted symptomatic. Finally, individuals who endorse at least three of the criteria in the non-addicted asymptomatic range (1 - 2 on the on the Likert scale) are classified as non-addicted asymptomatic. It has been shown that the scale possesses good internal reliability (α =. 78 to α =. 92) and test–retest reliability ($r = 0.92$).

4.5. LESS WIDELY USED TOOLS IN THE ASSESSMENT OF EXERCISE ADDICTION

Prior to the development of psychometrically validated tools for gauging exercise addiction, the condition was investigated with interviews (Sachs and Pargman, 1979) and the *Commitment to Running Scale* (CR – Carmack and Martens, 1979). However, using the CR has been criticized (Szabo et al., 1997), because addiction and commitment in exercise are two different constructs. While addiction is a dysfunction, commitment to exercise implies involvement in the activity for enjoyment and fun.

The *Negative Addiction Scale* (NAS – Hailey and Bailey, 1982) has been used primarily with runners. Its items measure the psychological rather than physiological aspects of compulsive running. Because of its mediocre psychometric characteristics, inference about scores that define a person as addicted to running is hard to be made.

The *Exercise Beliefs Questionnaire* (EBQ – Loumidis and Wells, 1998) assesses personal assumptions in exercise on the bases of four factors: 1) *social desirability*, 2) *physical appearance*, 3) *mental and emotional functioning*, and 4) *vulnerability to disease and aging*. The scale's internal reliability is relatively good, ranging between $\alpha = .67$ and $\alpha = .89$ and concurrent validity between $r = .67$ and $r = .77$).

Another instrument, the *Bodybuilding Dependency Scale* (BDS – Smith, Hale, and Collins, 1998), was developed specially to assess excessive exercise in bodybuilders. The questionnaire contains three subscales: 1) *social dependence* (individual's need to be in the weightlifting environment), 2) *training dependence* (individual's compulsion to lift weights) and 3) *mastery dependence* (individual's need to exert control over his/her training schedule). Because of its sports specificity the BDS has restricted range of employability in sport and exercise psychology.

4.5. Strengths and Limitations of Paper and Pencil Tools in Gauging Exercise Addiction

All exercise addiction questionnaires could only be used for surface screening or risk assessment but not for medical diagnosis. Therefore, the questionnaire method of assessment estimates the *likelihood of addiction* in the respondent. Even individuals scoring above average may not necessarily be addicted to exercise. Nevertheless, a score that is close to the maximum may suggest that there is a possibility or a high risk of addiction. For example, a score of 24 on the EAI needs to be considered as a potential warning sign. Still, the proper and unambiguous assessment of exercise addiction could only be established after a deep interview with a qualified health professional. Serving well for screening purposes, exercise addiction questionnaires direct the individual, or those who are concerned, in the right direction. In schools, sport and leisure facilities, they are quite useful for screening, but many addicted exercisers perform their activity in an informal setting, by simply going out for a run on their own. In fact, it is likely that most exercise addicts are loners in some sense because no structured physical activity classes or exercising friends could keep up with the massive amount and busy schedule of exercise in which they engage on a daily basis. Assuming that only about one to three percent of the exercising population may be affected by exercise addiction (Szabo, 2000, Terry et al., 2004) and that the majority of exercises addicts are "lone wolfs", the use of the questionnaires may have further limited value in assessment.

Although the assessment of exercise addiction is based on some general symptoms of addiction listed in the DSM IV (1994), the latter does not list exercise addiction as a separate category of dysfunction. There may be several reasons for the omission of exercises addiction from the DSM IV. First, the incidence of exercise addiction is very rare and ambigous. The estimation is based on a few case-studies that are occasionally reported in the literature (Szabo, 2000). Ensuing, there is perhaps insufficient medical or scientific evidence on which the DSM IV could draw solid conclusions. Second, in contrast to the passive and *let go / let down* attitude common in addictive behaviors, exercise addiction requires substantial physical and mental effort, determination, and self-discipline. These characteristics are positive that are in conflict with the *quick fix* aspects of other addictions. A third reason, that may also be true in other addictions, is that exercise addiction identified on the basis of certain symptoms, may only be a *symptom in itself* of an underlying psychological or mental dysfunction in which exercise abuse is a means of escape from the problem rather than the route of the problem. Accordingly, if exercise addiction is indeed escape from one or more unpleasant or noxious life event(s), the motivational incentives beyond this escape or avoidance behavior need to be examined more closely.

Chapter 5

MOTIVATIONAL INCENTIVES IN EXERCISE ADDICTION

At several places in this monograph it has been emphasized and re-emphasized that commitment to exercise is different from addiction to exercise, regardless of the amount of exercise. Motivation for exercise is another distinguishing characteristic between commitment and addiction. People exercise for specific reasons. The reason is often an intangible reward like being in shape, looking good, being with friends, staying healthy, building muscles, losing weight, etc. The personal experience of the anticipated reward strengthens the exercise behavior. Scholars known as behaviorists, adhering to one of the most influential schools of thought in the field of Psychology, postulate that behavior could be understood and explained through reinforcement and punishment. Accordingly, the *operant conditioning theory* suggests that there are three principles of behavior: *positive reinforcement, negative reinforcement*, and *punishment* (Bozarth, 1994). Positive reinforcement is a motivational incentive for doing something to *gain* a reward that is something pleasant or desirable (e.g., increased muscle tone). The reward then becomes a motivational incentive, which increases the likelihood of that behavior to reoccur. In contrast, negative reinforcement is a motivational incentive for doing something to *avoid* a noxious or unpleasant (e.g., gaining weight) event. The avoidance or reduction of the noxious stimulus is the reward, which then increases the probability of that behavior to reoccur. It should be noted that both positive and negative reinforcers increase the likelihood of the behavior (Bozarth, 1994), but their mechanism is different because in positive reinforcement there is a *gain following the action* (e.g. feeling revitalized), whereas in behaviors motivated by negative reinforcement one attempts to *avoid something bad or unpleasant before happening* that otherwise would occur (e.g. feeling guilty or fat if a planned exercise session is missed).

Punishment refers situations in which the imposition of some noxious or unpleasant stimulus or event or alternately the removal of a pleasant or desired stimulus or event reduces the probability of a given behavior to reoccur. In contrast to reinforcers, punishers suppress the behavior and, therefore, exercise or physical activity should never be used (by teachers, parents, or coaches) as punishment. Paradoxically, exercise addiction may be perceived as self-punishing behavior. It is a very rare form of addiction (compared to alcohol, tobacco or drug abuse) requiring substantial physical effort often to the point of exhaustion. Therefore, exercises addicts may be viewed as either masochistic or self-punishing individuals.

People addicted to exercise may be motivated by negative reinforcement (e.g., to avoid withdrawal symptoms) as well as positive reinforcement (e.g., *runner's high;* Pierce, 1994; Szabo, 1995). However, negative reinforcement, or avoidance behavior, is not a characteristic of the committed exercisers (Szabo, 1995). Indeed, committed exercisers maintain their exercise regimen for benefiting from the activity. On the other hand, addicted exercisers *have to do it* or else something will happen to them. Their exercise may be an "obligation" (also reflected by the popular term "obligatory exercise") that needs to be fulfilled or otherwise an unwanted life event could occur like the inability to cope with stress, or gaining weight, becoming moody, etc. Every time a person undertakes behavior to avoid something negative, bad, or unpleasant, the motive behind that behavior may be classified as negative reinforcement. In these situations the person involved *has to do it* in contrast to *wants to do it*.

There are many examples in other sport areas where a behavior initially driven by positive reinforcement may turn into negatively reinforced or motivated behavior. For example, an outstanding football player who starts playing the game for fun, after being discovered as a talent and being offered a service contract in a team, becomes a professional player who upon signing the contract *is expected* to perform. Although the player may still enjoy playing (especially when all goes well), the pressure or expectation to perform is the *"has to do"* new facet of football playing and the negatively reinforcing component of his (or her) sporting behavior. Table 1 illustrates the differences between the underlying motives in exercises behaviors driven by negative and positive reinforcement.

Duncan (1974) in relation to drug addiction purports that addiction is almost identical with, and semantically is just another name for, avoidance or escape behavior when the unpleasant feeling is being negatively reinforced by drug taking. People addicted to exercise, in this view, reach for a means - with which they had past relief-inducing experience - that provides them with temporary escape from an ongoing state of emotional distress and struggle, which might be caused by mental dysfunction, or by psychosocial stress, or by an aversive social or physical environment. In Duncan's view, all addictions represent similar negatively reinforced behaviors.

Duncan states that negative reinforcement is a powerful mechanism in maintaining high-frequency and long-persistent behaviors. Animals that could have escaped a noxious stimulus or event by pressing a bar (negative reinforcement) will often do so to the point of ignoring other even instinctual activities like eating, sleeping, sexual activity, etc. Avoidance behaviors are highly resistant to extinction and even when they appear to have been finally eliminated, they tend to reoccur spontaneously. Consequently, the relapse rate in addictions, regardless of the form of addiction, is very high. In Duncan's view, the intensity, compulsiveness, and proneness to relapse, that are important characteristics in addictions, result from the fact that the behavior is maintained by negative reinforcement.

Table 5.1: Exercise behaviors driven by positive and reinforcement.

Positive reinforcement	Negative reinforcement
Origin: Behaviorist school of thought. *Definition:* Positive Reinforcement strengthens behavior because a tangible or intangible *gain* is secured as a result of the behavior.	*Origin:* Behaviorist school of thought. *Definition:* Negative Reinforcement strengthens behavior because a negative condition is stopped and/or *avoided* as a consequence of the behavior.
Examples: "I feel revitalized after exercise" (*gains* good feeling) "I like to decrease my running time on the same distance. (*gains* skill and confidence) "I lift weights to look good." (*gains* physical benefits, good looks)	*Examples:* "I run *to avoid* circulatory problems that my parents had." "I go to gym *to avoid* getting fat." "I have to run my 10 miles every day, or else I feel guilty and irritated." (*avoids* feeling of guilt and irritation)

Although positive reinforcement like the runners' high and brain reward systems have been implicated in the explanation of exercise addiction, the motivational incentive in addiction may be more closely connected to prevention, escape, or avoidance of something unwanted as in some recent models of addiction (Baker et al., 2004). Accordingly, the process of addiction is more likely motivated by negative reinforcement in which the affected individual has to exercise to avoid an unwanted consequence.

Chapter 6

MODELS

6.0 – MODELS EXPLAINING EXERCISE ADDICTION

6.1. The Sympathetic Arousal Hypothesis

A physiological model suggesting how adaptation of the organisms to habitual exercise may lead to addiction is based a Thompson's and Blanton's (1987) work. From most exercise physiology textbooks it is known that regular exercise, especially aerobic exercise like running, if performed for a sustained period, results in decreased heart rate at rest. While heart rate is only a crude measure of the body's sympathetic activity (which is directed by the autonomic nervous system), it is, nevertheless, a sensitive measure and it is often used to mirror sympathetic activity. A lower resting heart rate after training results from the adaptation of the organism to exercise. Figure 6.1 illustrates a hypothetical case in which the exerciser's initial basal heart rate (red line) on the average is about 62 beats per minute (bpm). Every single session of exercise (green line) raises the heart rate to well above 100 bpm (depending on exercise intensity of course) that upon recovery - following exercise - returns lo lower than the pre-exercise or basal heart rate. With repeated exercise challenge, resulting from aerobic training, and a concomitantly more efficient cardiovascular system, the basal heart rate, partially reflecting sympathetic activity, decreases. Lower sympathetic activity at rest means lower level of arousal. This new arousal state may be experienced as lethargic or energy-lacking state, which according to Thomson's and Blanton's hypothesis urges the exercises to do something about it, or to increase her or his level of arousal. The obvious means to do that is exercise. However, the effects of exercise in increasing arousal are only temporary and, therefore, more and more bouts of exercise may be needed to achieve an optimal state of arousal. Furthermore, not only the frequency but also the intensity of exercise sessions may need to increase due to training effect. Such an increase accounts for the tolerance in the addiction process.

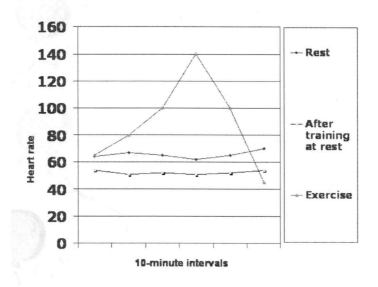

Figure 6.1. A hypothetical graph of how one's basal (resting) heart rate may decrease after prolonged aerobic training. Note that the green line illustrates the challenge in heart rate during one exercise session only. The adaptation, reflected by the difference between the red and the blue lines, may require several months and in some cases even longer.

Uncomfortable sensations of "non-optimal" level of arousal are a form of withdrawal feelings or symptoms that prompt the exerciser to get moving and engage in a workout. As the frequency of workouts and the reliance on exercise to regulate arousal increase, the behavior progressively assumes a central part in the exerciser's life, which is known as salience. When the need to exercise is not fulfilled, the addicted person could feel lethargic, lacking energy, guilty, irritated, etc. (see Figure 6.2). He or she has to exercise, as mentioned above, to avoid a bunch of uncomfortable feelings. At this point the exerciser loses control over her/his exercise, which is no longer performed for fun or pleasure, but a negatively reinforced obligation.

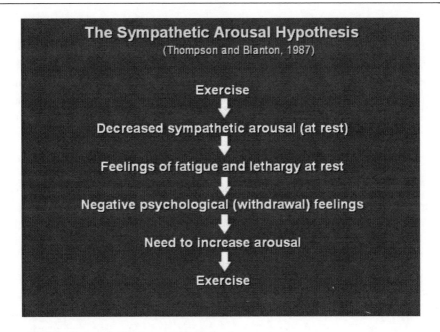

Figure 6.2. The Sympathetic Arousal Hypothesis.

6.2. The Cognitive Appraisal Hypothesis

There is psychological explanation for exercise addiction as well. Some exercisers try to escape from their psychological problems (Morris, 1989). They are very few in numbers and use exercise as a means of coping with stress. Like others, who turn to drugs and alcohol in difficult life situations, exercisers may abuse their exercise so that behavioral addiction becomes evident (Griffiths, 1997). However, because exercise, in contrast to alcohol or drugs, involves significant physical effort (Cockerill and Riddington, 1996) it is an inconvenient coping method that requires strong self-determination, self-discipline, and possibly a bit of masochistic attitude. Therefore, the incidence of exercise addiction is very rare in contrast to other forms of escape behaviors.

Szabo (1995) proposed a cognitive appraisal hypothesis for the better understanding of the psychological path in exercise addiction, as summarized in Figure 6.3. Accordingly, once the exerciser uses exercise as a coping method with stress, the affected individual starts to depend on exercise to function well. She or he believes that exercise is a healthy means of coping with stress based on information from scholastic and public media sources. Therefore, she or he uses rationalization to explain the exaggerated amount of exercise that progressively takes a tool on other obligations and daily activities. However, when the interference of exercise with other duties and tasks obliges the exerciser to reduce the amount of daily exercise, a psychological hardship emerges, which is manifested through a set of negative feelings like irritability, guilt, anxiousness, sluggishness, etc. These feelings collectively represent the withdrawal symptoms experienced because of no or less exercise. When exercise is used to cope with stress, apart the collection of negative psychological feeling states there is also a loss in the coping mechanism (exercise). Concomitantly, the exerciser loses control over the stressful situations that she or he used to deal with by resorting to exercise. The loss of the coping mechanism, followed by the loss of control over stress, generates an increased perception of vulnerability to stress, therefore further amplifying the negative psychological feelings associated with the lack of exercise. This problem could be resolved only through resuming the previous pattern of exercise at the expense of the other obligations in the daily life. Obviously, while exercise provides an instant reduction in the negative psychological feelings, the ignorance or superficial treatment of other social and work obligations results in conflict with people, possibly losses at work or school, or even loss of job, altogether causing further stress. The addicted exerciser is then trapped in a vicious circle needing more exercise to deal with the consistently increasing life-stress, part of which is caused by exercise itself.

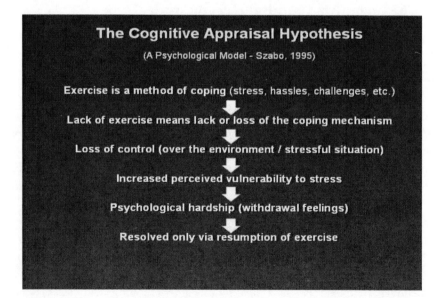

Figure 6.3. The Cognitive Appraisal Hypothesis.

6.3. The Affect Regulation Hypothesis

The affect regulation hypothesis states that exercise has dual effect on mood. First it increases positive affect (defined as: momentary psychological feeling states of longer persistence than momentary emotions) and, therefore, contributes to an improved general mood state (defined as: prolonged psychological feeling states lasting for several hours or even days). Second, it decreases negative affect or the temporary state of guilt, irritability, sluggishness, anxiety, etc. and, therefore, further contributes to an improved general mood state (Hamer and Karageorghis, 2007). However, the affect-regulating effects of exercise are temporary and the longer is the interval between two exercise sessions the experience of negative affect becomes increasingly likely. In fact after prolonged periods of abstention from exercise (which are prolonged only in relation to the busy exercise-schedule of the addicted person, since otherwise they are as short as 24 to 36 hours; Sachs, 1981), these negative affective states become severe deprivation sensations or withdrawal symptoms, which are relieved only through exercise. Therefore, as the cycle continues more and more exercise is needed to experience improvement in affect and general mood, and in parallel the inter-exercise rest period needs to decrease to prevent the surfacing of withdrawal symptoms.

6.4. The Thermogenic Regulation Hypothesis

This model is based on physiological evidence that physical exercise increases body temperature. A warm body temperature induces a relaxing state with concomitant reduction in anxiety (similar to sun-tanning, Turkish or warm bath, and sauna effects). Consequently, physical exercise reduces anxiety (De Vries, 1981; Morgan and O'Connor, 1988) whilst inducing relaxation as a consequence of increased body temperature. Lower levels of anxiety and higher states of relaxation act as positive reinforcers for the exercise behavior. The pleasant psychological state emerging from the relaxing and anxiety relieving effects of exercise, conditions (teaches) the person to resort to exercise when they experience anxiety. Higher levels of anxiety may be associated with the need for more exercise. Consequently, the duration or the intensity – or even both modalities – may be increased to obtain a stronger antidote to anxiety. The expectation of such dose-response relationship between exercise and anxiety eventually leads to tolerance that is another common characteristic in exercise addiction.

6.5. The Catecholamine Hypothesis

This hypothesis is based on the empirical observation that increased levels of catecholamines in the body may be observed after exercise (Cousineau et al., 1977). Catecholamines, among other functions, are heavily involved in the stress response and in the sympathetic response to exercise. In light of the catecholamine hypothesis, it is speculated that the central catecholaminergic activity is altered by exercise. Because central catecholamine levels are involved in regulating mood and affect and play an important role in mental dysfunctions like depression, the alteration of catecholamines by exercise is an attractive speculation. To date, however, there is inconclusive evidence to this surmise. Indeed, it is unclear whether the peripheral changes in catecholamines have an effect on brain catecholamine levels or vice versa. Furthermore, the changes in brain catecholamine levels during exercise in humans are unknown, because direct measurement in the human brain is not possible.

6.6. The Endorphin Hypothesis

This model is a very popular one in the literature because it is connected to the phenomenon of "runner's high" (defined again as: the pleasant feeling associated with positive self image, sense of vitality, control, and a sense of fulfillment reported by runners as well as by other exercisers after a certain amount and intensity of exercise. The feeling has been associated with increased levels of endogenous opioids and catecholamines observed after exercise). The surmise behind this model is that exercise leads to increased levels of endorphins in the brain, which act as internal psychoactive drugs yielding a sense of euphoria. In fact this hypothesis is analogous to substance or drug addiction (e.g. heroin, morphine, etc.) with the notable exception that the psychoactive agent (beta endorphin) is generated internally during exercise instead of being administered from the outside. This is an elegant model and if there were evidence for this hypothesis it would explain why exercise addicts would resort to exaggerated or even masochistic amounts of exercise to internally-generate the "drugs" that other addicts buy from dealers. Indeed, both the catecholamine hypothesis and the endorphin hypothesis have been implicated in the euphoric feeling of runners high. If exercise addiction could also be driven by positive reinforcement, then the most plausible explanation is the runner's high phenomenon. Consequently, this highly disputed but anecdotally repeatedly reported psychological feeling states needs to be evaluated.

THE RUNNER'S HIGH PHENOMENON

"I believe in the runner's high, and I believe that those who are passionate about running are the ones who experience it to the fullest degree possible. To me, the runner's high is a sensational reaction to a great run! It's an exhilarating feeling of satisfaction and achievement. It's like being on top of the world, and truthfully... there's nothing else quite like it!"

Sasha Azevedo

(http://www.runtheplanet.com/resources/historical/runquotes.asp)

For many decades, marathon runners, long distance joggers, and even average runners have reported a feeling of euphoria replacing the fatigue and pain of physical exertion caused by long sessions of exercise. Such euphoria triggers a sensation of "flying", effortless movement, and has become a legendary goal referred to as "the zone" (Goldberg, 1988). The runner's high phenomenon has been closely linked to exercises addiction. The existence of runner's high is subject of heated debate in the scientific and scholastic circles. The question is whether a biochemical explanation for the runner's high exists, or it is a purely psychologically conceptualized and popularized terminology. Exercise addiction, if driven by positive reinforcement, would require an explanation that has physiological and biochemical foundations. Runners (and most habitual exercisers) experience withdrawal symptoms when their exercise is prevented. The symptoms include guilt, irritability, anxiety, and other unpleasant feelings (Szabo, 1995). Research shows that the human body produces its own opiate-like peptides, called endorphins, and like morphine, these peptides could cause dependence (Farrell, Gates, Maksud, and Morgan, 1982) and, consequently, may be the route of withdrawal symptoms. In general, endorphins are known to be responsible for pain and pleasure responses in the central nervous system. Morphine and other exogenous opiates *bind to the same receptors* that the body intended for endogenous opioids or endorphins, and since morphine's analgesic and euphoric effects are well documented, comparable effects for endorphins could be anticipated (Sforzo, 1988).

Research has been conducted to examine the effects of fitness levels, gender, and exercise intensity on endogenous opioid – mainly beta-endorphin – production during cycling, running on a treadmill, participating in aerobic dance, and running marathons. Biddle and Mutrie (1991) reported research that has shown that aerobic exercise could cause beta-endorphin levels to increase fivefold in contrast to baseline levels. Fitness levels of the research participants appears to be irrelevant as both trained and untrained individuals experience an increase in beta-endorphin levels, although the metabolism of beta-endorphins appears to be more efficient in trained athletes (Goldfarb and Jamurtas, 1997).

A decade ago, Goldfarb et al. (1998) researched gender differences in beta-endorphin production during exercise. Their results could not reveal gender-differences in beta-endorphin response to exercise. Other studies have demonstrated that both exercise intensity and duration are factors in increasing beta-endorphin concentrations. For example, the exercise needs to be performed at above 60% of the individual's maximal oxygen uptake (VO_2 max; Goldfarb and Jamurtas 1997) and for at least 3 minutes (Kjaer and Dela, 1996) to detect changes in endogenous opioids.

Researchers have further examined these findings by examining the correlation between exercise-induced increase in beta-endorphin levels and mood changes using the Profile of Mood States (POMS) inventory (Farrell et al., 1982). The POMS was administered to all participants before and after their exercise session. Respondents give numerical ratings to five negative categories of mood (tension, depression, anger, fatigue and confusion) and one positive category (vigor). Adding the five negative affect scores and then subtracting from the total the vigor score yields a "total mood disturbance" (TMD) score. In Farrell's study the TMD scores improved by 15 and 16 raw score units from the baseline, after subjects exercised at 60% and 80% VO_2 max. Quantitatively, mood improved about 50%, which corresponds to clinical observations that people's moods are elevated after vigorous exercise workouts. Farrell et al. (1982) using radioimmunoassay also observed two- to fivefold increase in plasma beta-endorphin concentrations as measured before and after exercise.

However, Farrell et al.'s research is inconclusive. First, only six well-trained endurance athletes were studied and the six showed large individual variations in beta-endorphin response to submaximal treadmill exercise. Second, the exercise-induced changes in mood scores were not statistically significantly different between pre- and post-exercises scores. Third, no significant relationship between

mood measures obtained with the POMS inventory and plasma beta-endorphin levels were found. Therefore, the obtained results cannot prove conclusively that beta-endorphins cause mood elevations. A more questionable issue, however, also recognized by Farrell et al. is that the beta-endorphin measures in the experiment comes from plasma - which means that this type of beta-endorphin is located in the periphery. Because of its chemical makeup, beta-endorphin cannot cross the blood brain barrier (BBB). Hence, plasma beta-endorphin fluctuations do not reflect beta-endorphin fluctuations in the brain. Some researchers have speculated that endogenous opiates in the plasma may act centrally and therefore can be used to trace CNS activity (Biddle and Mutrie, 1991). At this time, such a surmise concerning beta-endorphins could only rely on circumstantial evidence that met-enkephalin and dynorphin two opioids, which show a modification mechanism that could possibly transport them across the BBB (Sforzo, 1988). Unfortunately, direct measurement of changes in brain beta-endorphins involves cutting open the brain and doing radioimmunoassay on brain slices. Animal studies, using rats, have been performed and they have shown an increase in opioid receptor binding after exercise (Sforzo, Seeger, Pert, Pert, and Dotsen, 1986).

In humans, to work around this problem, researchers proposed that naloxone could be a useful in testing whether beta-endorphins played a role in CNS-mediated responses like euphoria and analgesia. Since it is a potent opioid receptor antagonist, it competes with beta-endorphin to bind the same receptor. Thus, injection of naloxone into humans should negate the euphoric and analgesic effects produced by exercise, if beta-endorphin perpetrates such effects indeed. It was found that naloxone decreased the analgesic effect reportedly caused by runner's high, but other researchers who conducted similar experiments remain divided about these results. As for naloxone's effects on mood elevation, Markoff, Ryan and Young (1982) observed that naloxone did not reverse the positive mood changes induced by exercise.

Mounting evidence demonstrates that beta-endorphins are not necessary for the euphoria experienced by exercisers. Harte, Eifert, and Smith (1995) noted that although exercise produces both positive emotions and a rise in beta-endorphin levels, the two are not necessarily connected. Indeed, physically undemanding activities like watching humor or listening to music produce identical elevations in mood to exercise (Szabo, 2006; Szabo, Aisnsworth, and Danks 2005) although accompanying elevations in beta-endorphins could not be observed after humor (Berk et al., 1989) or music (McKinney, Tims, Kumar and Kumar, 1997). Similarly, Harte et al. (1995) found that both running and meditation resulted in significant positive changes in mood. In addition to taking mood measures, Harte et al. have also measured plasma beta-endorphin levels of the participants. As expected, those in the meditation group did not show a rise in beta-endorphin levels in spite of reported elevations in mood. Such results seem to further question the link between mood improvement and changes in beta-endorphin levels after exercise.

Answering the improved mood and increased beta-endorphin levels connection question inversely, experiments were carried out in which beta-endorphin was directly injected into the bloodstream of healthy participants. The results failed to show any changes in mood (Biddle and Mutrie, 1991). On the other hand, beta-endorphin injections had a positive effect on clinically depressed patients (Biddle and Mutrie, 1991). Further, electroconvulsive therapy, used to treat patients with depression, also increased plasma b-endorphin levels.

The lack of beta-endorphin release during meditation and the lack of mood alteration after beta-endorphin injection, call for attention on factors that influence beta-endorphin levels. In an effort to consolidate peripheral beta-endorphin data with the central nervous effects, researchers have realized that the peripheral opioid system requires further investigation. Taylor et al. (1994) proposed that during exercise acidosis is the trigger of beta-endorphin secretion in the bloodstream. Their results showed that blood pH level strongly correlated with the beta-endorphin levels (acidic conditions raise the concentration of b-endorphin, buffering the blood attenuates this response). The explanation behind such observations is that acidosis increases respiration and stimulates a feedback inhibition mechanism in the form of beta-endorphin. The latter interacts with neurons responsible for respiratory control, and beta-endorphin, therefore, serves the purpose of preventing hyperventilation (Taylor et al., 1994). How is then this physiological mechanism connected to CNS-mediated emotional responses? Sforzo (1988) noted that since opioids have inhibitory functions in the CNS, if a system is to be activated through opioids at least one other neural pathway must be involved. Thus, instead of trying to establish how peripheral amounts of beta-endorphin act on the CNS, researchers could develop an alternate physiological model demonstrating how the emotional effects of opioids may be activated through the inhibition of the peripheral sympathetic activity (Sforzo, 1988).

While the "runner's high" phenomenon may never be empirically established as a fact and beta-endorphins' importance in this event is questionable, other studies have shown how peripheral beta-endorphins affect centrally-mediated behavior. Electro-acupuncture used to treat morphine addiction by diminishing cravings and relieving withdrawal symptoms, caused b-endorphin levels to rise (McLachlan, Hay, and Coleman, 1994). Since exercise also increases beta-endorphin levels in the plasma, McLachlan et al. (1994) investigated whether exercise could lower exogenous opiate intake. Rats were fed morphine and methadone for several days and then randomly divided into two groups of exercisers and non-exercisers. At that time, voluntary exogenous opiate intake was recorded to see if the exercise would affect the consumption of opiate in exercising rats. The results showed that while opiate consumption has increased in both groups, exercising rats did not consume as much as non-exercising animals and the difference was statistically significant (McLachlan et al., 1994). These findings suggest that exercise does decrease craving.

In conclusion, the connection between beta-endorphins, runner's high, and exercise addiction remains an elegant explanation without sufficient empirical support. It is likely that the intense positive emotional experience, to which athletes, runners, and scientist refer as runner's high, is evoked by several mechanisms acting jointly. Szabo (2006) has shown that while exercises and humor are equally effective in decreasing negative mood and increasing positive mood, the effects of exercise last longer than that of humor. These results are evidence for the involvement of more than one mechanism in mood alterations after physically active and relatively passive interventions. With reference to exercise addiction, although intensive positive feelings may be motivational factors to indulge in more and more exercise, when the exerciser loses control over her/his exercise (that happens in addiction by definition) the activity becomes an obligation. It has to be performed or else craving or withdrawal symptoms interfere with the normal functioning of the individual. Consequently, while the runner's high may be a factor at the onset of exercise addiction, the maintenance of this compulsive behavior occurs via negative, rather than positive reinforcement. It is reasonable to conclude then, that the runner's high phenomenon is only weakly or distantly associated with exercise addiction.

Chapter 8

CORRELATES OF EXERCISE ADDICTION

Researchers have looked at the correlates of exercise addiction but have been unable to identify when or why a transition takes place from "healthy" to "unhealthy" exercise behavior (Johnson, 1995). Exercise addiction appears to be positively related to anxiety (Morgan, 1979; Rudy and Estok, 1989) and negatively related to self-esteem (Estok and Rudy, 1986; Rudy and Estok, 1989). Further, the length of experience with a particular physical activity appears to be positively associated with exercise addiction (Furst and Germone, 1993; Hailey and Bailey, 1982; Thaxton, 1982). If experience is associated with exercise addiction, it is reasonable to speculate that a major life event change (or stress) may trigger addiction that is evinced through "revolutionary" rather than evolutionary changes in the habitual physical activity pattern of the individual. The affected individual may see this form of coping as healthy on the basis of popular knowledge and the media-spread information about the positive aspects of exercise.

Indeed, the media plays an important role in what people believe about and expect from their exercise. The media-propagated positive image of the exercising individual provides a mask behind which some exercisers with severe emotional distress may hide. Thus the media-projected positive information about physical activity could be used to deny the existence of the problem (a characteristic of addictive behaviors) and to delay its detection to the advanced stages when all symptoms of addiction are vividly present. Because of such a possible delay, it is likely that only case studies, presented in the literature, reflect genuine cases of exercise addiction. Indeed, a random sample of habitual exercisers may contain very few cases, if any (!), of exercise addicts (Morris, 1989).

RESEARCH

9.0 – RESEARCH ON EXERCISE ADDICTION

"I moved to a new town and decided to join a health club as a way of meeting people. Soon, exercise began to become a focal part of my life and I became more determined to keep fit and improve my physique. Gradually the three hours a day I was doing increased to six hours and I started to become totally obsessive about exercise. I wouldn't miss a day at the gym. I just lost sight of my body really - I just had to do my workout, come what may, and get my fix."

(Source: Evening Standard, 01/08/2000).

9.1. Personality-Oriented Research

Personality-oriented research or the trait approach is based on the assumption that aberrant or pathological personality characteristics, like obsessive-compulsiveness and narcissism, are instrumental in the etiology of exercise addiction. Researchers are trying to identify those personality characteristics that predispose an individual to exercise addiction. Investigators in this area are faced with several difficulties around the definition and assessment of exercise addiction as well as around the general difficulty in personality research in disentangling stable from changeable characteristics.

In an early widely cited but relatively controversial study, Yates, Leehay and Shisslak (1983) suggested that addicted male runners resembled patients suffering of anorexia nervosa on certain personality dispositions (introversion, inhibition of anger, high expectations, depression, and excessive use of denial) and labeled this resemblance as the anorexia-analogue hypothesis. To test their hypothesis Yates et al. examined the personality characteristics of 60 male heavy exercisers and contrasted their responses to those commonly reported by patients diagnosed with anorexia nervosa. While supporting data were not provided, Yates et al. claimed that running and extreme dieting were both dangerous attempts to establish an identity, as either addicted to exercise or as anorexic. This research has been severely criticized for a number of shortcomings including the lack of supporting data, poor methodology, lack of relevance to the average runner, over-reliance on extreme cases or individuals, and exaggerating the similarities between the groups (Blumenthal, O'Toole, and Chang, 1984). Indeed, subsequent research has failed to show undisputable commonalities between the personality characteristics of people affected by exercise addiction and those suffering of eating disorders (e.g., Blumenthal et al., 1984; Coen and Ogles, 1993). Consequently, the anorexia analogue hypothesis for a substantial period was seen as only speculative and has failed to gather empirical support.

In another early study Estok and Rudy (1986) examined 57 marathon and 38 non-marathon female runners on physical (e.g., shin splints and knee or hip pain) and psychosocial symptoms (e.g., anxiety and self-esteem), as well as addictive behaviors using a 14-item questionnaire developed by the authors themselves. The results revealed that marathon runners scored significantly higher on addictive behaviors in comparison to the non-marathon runners. The frequency of injuries among marathon runners was also significantly higher than in non-marathon runners. However, the authors attributed the differences in the incidence of injuries to the actual differences in running distance between the two groups and not to the level of addiction to running. Although no differences, between the marathon and non-marathon running groups, for psychological symptoms were found, there was a negative correlation between addiction scores and self-esteem, suggesting proneness to addiction in people with low self-esteem.

Yates et al. (1992) investigated the personality characteristics of male and female runners who ran a minimum of 15 miles (24 km) per week. According to participants' responses on an 18-item exercise addiction questionnaire developed by the authors, and on the basis of a semi-structured interview, runners could be classified as either obligatory (addicted) or non-obligatory (not addicted) exercisers. Ten male and 17 female participants were classified as obligatory runners, while the non-obligatory group comprised 20 males and 19 females. Participants completed the Profile of Mood States (POMS) inventory (McNair, Lorr, and Droppleman, 1981), the Eysenck Personality Questionnaire (Eysenck and Eysenck, 1991), the Minnesota Multiphasic Personality Inventory (Dahlstrom and Welch, 1960), the Bem Sex Role Inventory (Bem, 1981), the Internal-

External Locus of Control Scale (Rotter, 1966), the Eating Attitudes Test (Garner and Garfinkel, 1979), and the Beck Depression Inventory (Beck, Ward, Mendelson, Mock, Erbaugh, 1961). Yates et al. found that obligatory runners were more likely to follow a strict diet, be preoccupied with their body, run alone, and report more positive changes in self-concept and control over their lives since taking up running than the non-obligatory runners. Further, the obligatory male runners were twice as likely to obtain elevated scores on the Minnesota Multiphasic Personality Inventory (MMPI) compared to the non-obligatory male runners. Therefore, Yates et al. have found some limited evidence for differences in personality measures of addicted and non-addicted runners.

Davis, Brewer, and Ratusny (1993) investigated the relationships between personality characteristics of addiction, obsessive-compulsiveness, and exercise addiction with exercise behavior. They tested 185 physically active male and female participants who completed the Commitment to Exercise Scale (Davis et al., 1993), the Addiction Scale (Eysenck and Eysenck, 1991), the Obsessive-Compulsive Personality Scale (Lazare, Klerman, and Armour, 1966), and the Drive for Thinness, Body Dissatisfaction, and Bulimia Subscales of the Eating Disorder Inventory (Garner, Olmsted, and Polivy, 1983). Participants were also interviewed about their exercise history over the past year. Davis et al. found that obsessive-compulsive personality characteristics in males were positively related to exercise frequency. In contrast to their hypothesis, exercise frequency was inversely related to addictiveness. Therefore, the hypothesized positive relationships between obsessive-compulsiveness, addictiveness, exercise addiction, and exercise behavior could not be demonstrated.

Coen and Ogles (1993) further examined the anorexia analogue hypothesis and tested the personality characteristics believed to be common to anorexics and runners (e.g., anxiety, perfectionism, and ego identity). A sample of 142 male marathon runners completed the Obligatory Exercise Questionnaire (Thompson and Pasman, 1991), the Multidimensional Perfectionism Scale (Frost, Marten, Lahart, and Rosenblate, 1990), the Trait Subscale of the State-Trait Anxiety Inventory (Speilberger, Gorsuch, Lushene, Vagg, and Jacobs, 1983), the Ego Identity Scale (Tan, Kendis, Fine, and Porac, 1977), and a short demographic questionnaire on running characteristics. A median split on the Obligatory Exercise Questionnaire was used to classify runners as either obligatory or non-obligatory using Yates et al.'s terminology for addiction to running. The authors have found that the obligatory (addicted) runners have reported more perfectionist characteristics compared to the non-obligatory runners. Specifically, obligatory runners were more concerned about making mistakes, have set higher personal standards for themselves, had more doubts about their actions, and had a higher need for organization than their non-obligatory runners. Obligatory runners also reported greater trait anxiety compared to the non-obligatory group. On the basis of these findings it was concluded that the anorexia analogue hypothesis was partially supported because only some of the personality characteristics proposed by Yates et al. (1983) were associated indeed with addictive running.

Later, in contrast to the study by Coen and Ogles (1993), Iannos and Tiggemann (1997) failed to disclose personality differences between addicted to exercise and non-addicted individuals. They examined 205 male and female participants who were divided into three groups according to the number of hours they exercised per week: light (0 to 5 hours), medium or moderate (5 to 11 hours), and excessive (more than 11 hours). The participants completed an author-developed questionnaire, which assessed their level of exercise addiction, the Rosenberg Self-esteem Scale (Rosenberg, 1965), the Internality Subscale of the Locus of Control Inventory (Levenson, 1981), the Obsessive-Compulsive Scale (Gibb, Bailey, Best, and Lambrinth, 1983), and the Drive for Thinness and Bulimia Subscales of the Eating Disorder Inventory. The results showed that excessive exercisers reported more disordered eating behaviors than the light and moderate exercisers. Further, women scored higher than men. In spite of the relationship between the amount of exercise and disordered eating, statistically no significant differences were found between the amount of exercise and the personality characteristics of self-esteem, locus of control, and obsessive-compulsiveness. These authors concluded that high volumes of exercise alone could not be connected with a pathological personality.

Hagan and Hausenblas (2003) examined the relationship between exercise addiction scores and perfectionism. They tested 79 university students who completed self-report measures of their exercise behavior, perfectionism, and exercise dependence symptoms. The authors have found that participants with high exercise addiction scores reported more perfectionism and larger volumes of exercise than participants with low scores of exercise addiction. The connection between perfectionism and exercises addiction warrants further investigation, because it may yields at least a partial answer to why exercise addicts, investing tremendous energy in their addiction, differ from other addicts who resort to "easy to reach" means to satisfy their cravings.

In a later study, Hausenblas and Giacobbi (2004) focused on the proposed link between a number of specific dimensions of personality (neuroticism, extraversion, agreeableness, openness, conscientiousness) and exercise addiction. They hypothesized that there would be a positive correlation between exercise addiction and neuroticism. Hausenblas and Giacobbi tested 390 university students. The participants completed several inventories including the NEO Five

Factor Inventory (Costa and McCrae, 1992) used to measure the levels of five personality dimensions (neuroticism, extraversion, openness, agreeableness, and conscientiousness), the Exercise Dependence Scale (EDS - Hausenblas and Symons Downs, 2002b) to assess symptoms of exercise addiction, the Leisure Time Exercise Questionnaire (Godin and Shephard, 1985) to gauge leisure activities, and the Drive for Thinness Scale (Garner, 1991) that was actually a subscale of the Eating Disorder Inventory-2 (Garner, 1991). The results of this study showed that proneness to exercise addiction, as based on the EDS scores, were positively correlated with neuroticism and extraversion while being negatively correlated with agreeableness. Openness and conscientiousness were unrelated failed to exercise addiction scores.

Summing up the research effort on the connection between exercise addiction and personality, it is clear that causal relationship has not been demonstrated. Any linkages between the two variables are correlational rather than causal in nature. The observed group differences (high versus low addiction scores) are inconsistent and they could be traced to many factors associated with exercise history and experience as well as beliefs and expectations associated with exercise. The popularity of investigations into personality and exercise addiction could be explained by the convenience of research in this area, relying on questionnaire data, and scholars' eagerness to pinpoint a consistent and common characteristic among exercise addicts that could be conceived as a warning sign in the etiology of exercise addiction.

9.2. Beta-Endorphin and Exercise Addiction Research

Only one study, published 15 years ago, has examined the link between beta-endorphins and exercise addiction. The study was based on previously published evidence (e.g. Farrell et al., 1982) that there is a considerable increase beta-endorphin levels after exercise, especially aerobic activities. Then, Pierce et al. (1993) studied the connection between plasma beta-endorphin levels and proneness to exercise addiction in eight women who trained in aerobic dance. The participants completed an exercise addiction assessment prior to taking part in a 45-minute session of continuous aerobic dance. Plasma beta-endorphin concentrations were measured both before and after the exercise session. The results revealed that mean plasma beta-endorphin levels were statistically significantly higher after the exercise in comparison to pre-exercise levels. The percent change scores (difference scores) between pre- and post-exercise beta-endorphin levels were then correlated with the exercise addiction scores. The result of the correlation was statistically not significant. Consequently, the research concludes that exercise addiction is not related to changes in plasma beta-endorphin levels after aerobic exercise.

9.3. Preponderance of Exercise Addiction

A common question posed by scientist and media reporters pertains to the prevalence of exercise addiction. The question is valid given that substantial research attention has been dedicated to the issue. Empirical research on the preponderance of exercise addiction is limited. The author is only aware of a few studies that could possibly provide an answer. The first account by Thornton and Scott (1995) projects an inflated figure. These authors examined a group pf 40 runners who were, on average, running over 40 miles per week. Using the Commitment to Running Scales (Carmack and Martens, 1979) the results revealed that 77% of the sample of runners studied could be classified as moderately or highly addicted to running. The authors have found that the predominant personal motives for the studied runners were related to mastery, competition, and weight regulation, although health concerns and fitness were also important incentives. The commitment to running scores, that were interpreted as addiction indices by the authors, were related to the frequency of running and distances run, but not to the number of years of running. A regression analyses showed that mastery and social recognition were key predictors of the levels of running commitment. The authors suggested those runners who start running for health promotion or maintenance, there is a potential risk of developing an obsessive commitment to running, and this may be more likely for those who are prone to stress. A major problem with this study is that the authors equated high levels of commitment to running with exercise addiction, which in fact was proven to represent two unrelated concepts (Szabo et al., 1996).

Two studies looked at the incidence of classifiable cases during the development and validation of two different exercise addiction questionnaires. Using the Exercise Dependence Scale (EDS) Hausenblas and Symons Downs (2002) identified that 2.5% of the studied sample could be classified as being addicted to exercise. Similarly, Terry, Griffiths and Szabo (2004), in the course of development of the Exercise Addiction Inventory (EAI), reported that 3.0% of the sample could be identified as at risk of exercise addiction. The two questionnaires, the EDS and the EAI, are highly correlated ($r = 0.81$; $p < 0.001$) with each other. The rates of exercise addiction reported in conjunction with the development of the EDS and EAI are low, supporting the argument that exercise addiction is rare

(Szabo, 2000; De Coverley Veale, 1995). Indeed, a later study substantiated the validity of such estimates about the preponderance of exercise addiction.

Szabo and Griffiths (2007) examined the prevalence of self-reported symptoms of exercise addiction in sport sciences students at a British university and in a sample drawn from the general exercising population. A total of 455 participants (261 sports science students and 194 controls) completed the Exercise Addiction Inventory (EAI – Terry, Szabo, and Griffiths, 2004). The sport science students had significantly higher mean scores on the EAI than exercisers from the general population. It was also found that 6.9% (18 out of 261) sport science students were possibly addicted to exercise, since they scored 24 or more on the EAI, compared to only 3.6% (7 out of 194) of the general exercising population, a result that approached ($p < 0.09$) but it did not reach the conservative level ($p < .05$) statistical significance. The findings of Szabo and Griffiths raise the possibility that sports science students may be more susceptible to exercise addiction than exercisers in the general population. At the same time, their findings confirm, that the preponderance of exercise addiction in the general exercising population is about 3% to 4%.

It should be noted that exercise addiction questionnaire only assess the risk or likelihood of exercise addiction. Consequently, questionnaires alone cannot be considered as diagnostic tools. The genuine cases of exercise addiction cannot be identified through scientific research. They surface occasionally in medical practices when the psychological burden or physical injury forces the affected person to seek help. Therefore, the 3% or near estimates of exercise addiction in the exercising population may be a very crude index and only represent high risk cases rather than actually diagnosed cases.

9.4. Case Studies of Exercise Addiction

Griffiths (1997) presents the only case study published in a scholastic paper. Joanne, aged 25, did not see herself as addicted to exercise, though her habit took up several hours of each day, occupied her thoughts continuously, and the craving for exercise had even forced her to walk out of university exams. She was obsessed with exercise, mostly a type of martial arts, but any form of exercise would do. Joanne described the buzz resulting from exercise as a feeling like being on amphetamines. With time she had developed a tolerance for exercise, and therefore she had to increase the volume of her exercise continuously to feel all right and to function normally. If she could not fulfil her need to exercise, she would get anxious and irritable, and suffered of headaches and nausea. She has spent money beyond her means to fund her habit, and has lost friends and even her partner to it. Joanne's case illustrates how the exercise addict loses control over her exercise and the extreme negative life events that may have permanent consequences, like abandoning an exam or losing a partner.

Another exercise addiction case, voluntarily shared with the public by the affected person, was published in the London *Evening Standard*, (August 01, 2000): Jackie Pugsley enjoyed her job as a schoolteacher. She had never been particularly sporty at school but in her twenties she started making up for lost time, taking up sports including tennis, squash, aerobics, badminton and circuit training, to help kick-start her social life. What started as a hobby became an obsession, until she became so addicted to exercise that she was forced to give up her work. The 36-year-old was the first person to complete the treatment programme at The Priory Hospital Bristol in 1996. Jackie described her obsession with exercise: "*I moved to a new town and decided to join a health club as a way of meeting people. Soon, exercise began to become a focal part of my life and I became more determined to keep fit and improve my physique. Gradually the three hours a day I was doing increased to six hours and I started to become totally obsessive about exercise. I wouldn't miss a day at the gym. I just lost sight of my body really - I just had to do my workout, come what may, and get my fix.*" At the height of her addiction Jackie was exercising for up to eight hours a day, starting with two hours on her exercise bike before work. She would walk for an hour at lunchtime, and then head off for a two-hour run after work, followed by a three-hour workout at the gym. Holidays would be spent at health farms and she would even get out the exercise bike on Christmas Day. Her dress size dropped from 14 to eight, and her weight slipped down to seven stone (and she is more than 5 ft 8in). "*I stopped doing the sports I actually enjoyed and was fixated about high-impact aerobic exercise. Instead of using sport to enhance my social life, I was becoming more and more isolated and was not enjoying the exercise at all*". By the time Jackie was admitted to hospital the regime had taken a physical toll. A combination of severe cramps and low blood pressure meant she was unable to walk for 10 days. "*Even though I was in agony I had to be sedated because I couldn't cope without the exercise. I had grown so acclimatized to pain that I didn't even question it. I had my amount of workout that I had to do. I might have spent the evening in the gym and been so exhausted that I would just about be able to climb the stairs - it didn't matter. Once I was inside I made myself spend another hour on my exercise bike.*" After several relapses Jackie was able to manage her addiction, although she was still seeing a psychiatrist for a while.

Joanne and Jackie's cases illustrate vividly the potentially irreversible negative consequences of exercise addiction. Cases like theirs do not surface in a randomly studied research sample; instead they may appear in medical practices. The affected individuals may seek medical help only when the negative consequences, resulting from excessive exercise, already took a toll on their lives and any further lengthening of the cycle could result in severe or even deadly consequences. Such diagnosed cases cannot be studied with questionnaires on which the bulk of exercise addiction literature is based. Nonetheless, paper and pencil tools, yielding knowledge about personality characteristics, needs and desires of people, could assess the potential risk for exercise addiction. As such research into exercise addiction is of paramount importance for prevention. From, the previous section it is known that only a small fraction of the exercising population may be affected by exercise addiction (3-4%), then one may question the effort invested in this area of research. However, considering that the consequences of exercise addiction may be life threatening, all effort invested in knowledge to be used for timely prevention is justified. Indeed, the 3-4% figure may seem to be small. However, the 3% figure is large if one considers that the exercising population is growing consistently as illustrated by data that in 2003 one third (33%) of the adult population in the United States (U.S.) engaged regularly in moderate physical activity (more than 30 minutes at least 5 times a week). It is noteworthy to mention that the U.S. target for 2010 is 50% (U.S. Department of Health and Human Services, 2004). Therefore, the number of those who statistically may be affected by exercise addiction (around the whole world) could be counted in millions. Should then there be a stronger justification for continued research effort in this area?

9.5. Exercise Addiction and Withdrawal Symptoms

Szabo (1995, 2000) claimed that all exercisers experience withdrawal symptoms at times when exercise is not possible for interfering reasons. He stressed, however, that those who are addicted to exercise would experience stronger deprivation sensations than those who are simply highly committed to exercise. Aidman and Woollard (2003) reported results that seem to provide support for Szabo's contention. They tested the connection of exercise addiction to mood and resting heart rate response to a 24-hour exercise deprivation from scheduled training in competitive runners. Sixty competitive runners, who had been training at least five times a week, were randomly assigned into an experimental (exercise-deprived) and a control group. Participants completed the Profile of Mood States (POMS) inventory, the Running Addiction Scale (RAS), and provided resting heart rate (RHR) measurements. Half of the participants missed the next scheduled training (exercise-deprived group), while the other half continued to train uninterruptedly (controls). Both groups completed again the POMS and provided RHR within 24 hours after the experiment. The results showed that the exercise-deprived group reported substantial withdrawal symptoms of depressed mood, reduced vigor and increased tension, anger, fatigue and confusion (measured by POMS), as well as significantly elevated RHR, within 24 hours after the missed training session. The control group showed no changes in mood or RHR. More importantly, the observed negative changes in mood and RHR response in the exercise-deprived group were associated with exercise addiction scores. Those who scored under the median experienced significantly less mood change and RHR shifts than hose with addiction scores above the median. Further, correlations between addiction scores and magnitude of increases in tension, anger, confusion, depression and RHR ranged from $r = 0.46$ to $r = 0.58$. The authors concluded that exercise addiction scores in habitual exercisers are associated with emotional and heart rate responses to exercise deprivation, indicating that the magnitude of these responses may, in turn, serve as early markers of exercise addiction. In accord with Szabo (1995, 2000) the severity of withdrawal symptoms is an important index for differentiating committed exercisers from those who re addicted.

Chapter 10

EXERCISE ADDICTION
AND EATING DISORDERS

De Coverley Veale (1987) differentiated between primary and secondary exercise dependence. In the previous sections primary dependence was examined. Secondary exercise dependence is a common characteristic of eating disorders such as Anorexia Nervosa and Bulimia Nervosa (De Coverley Veale, 1987). In these disorders, excessive exercise is considered to be an auxiliary feature used in caloric control and weight loss. Secondary exercise dependence occurs in different "doses" in people affected by eating disorders. It was estimated that one third of anorectics may be affected (Crisp, Hsu, Harding, and Hartshorn, 1980).

10.1. The Relationship between Exercise Addiction and Eating Disorders

A team of long-distance runners published the founding work in this area. This work has been briefly mentioned in the personality and exercise addiction section, but because it marks the foundation of research into exercise addiction and eating disorders it needs to be briefly re-introduced in this section as well. Yates et al. (1983) were themselves runners and at the same time scholars specialized in eating disorders. They observed a striking resemblance between the psychology of anorectic patients and the very committed runners with whom they run. They labeled this group of runners as obligatory runners. In the course of their research they interviewed sixty marathoners and closely examined the traits of a subgroup of male athletes who corresponded to the "obligatory" category. They reported that male obligatory runners resembled anorexic women in some personality traits, such as expression of anger, high self-expectation, tolerance of pain, and depression as well as in some demographic details. Yates et al. (1983) related these observations to a unique and hazardous way of establishment of self-identity. This work has marked the foundation of research into the relationship between exercise and eating disorders.

10.2. The Analogy between Anorexia and Excessive Exercising

Since Yates et al. (1983) published their article, a large number of studies have examined the relationship between exercise and eating disorders. A close examination of these studies (Table 10.1) reveals some opposing findings to the original report. For example, three studies comparing anorectic patients with high level, or obligatory, exercisers (Blumenthal, O'Toole and Chang, 1984; Davis et al., 1995; Knight, Schocken, Powers, Feld, and Smith, 1987) failed to demonstrate an analogy between anorexia and excessive exercising. The differences in methodology between these inquiries are, however, significant. They all looked for an analogy between excessive exercise and anorexia, but from a different perspective. Blumenthal et al. (1984) and Knight et al. (1987) examined a mixed gender sample's scores on a popular personality test (the Minnesota Multiphasic Personality Inventory - MMPI). Davis et al. (1995) tested an all female sample using specific questionnaires aimed at assessing compulsiveness, commitment to exercise, and eating disorders. Finally, Yates et al. (1983) looked to some demographic and personality parallels between obligatory runners and anorectic patients. Further, the classification of the exercise behavior may have differed in these studies. Therefore, these studies are not easily comparable.

Table 10.1. A summary table on research into exercise addiction and eating disorders

Author(s)	Participants	Objectives	Measurements	Conclusion about the relationship between exercise and eating disorders
Ackard, Brehm, and Steffen (2002)	586 female university students	to examine the connection between excessive exercise, disordered eating and a number of psychologic	Obligatory Exercise Questionnaire, Eating Disorders Inventory, The Center for Epidemiological Studies-Depression scale, Trait Meta-Mood	One group clearly manifested eating disorder traits and behaviors, as well as signs of psychological disturbance. Another group who exercised with equal intensity but less emotional fixation showed the fewest signs of eating disorders and psychological distress.

Author(s)	Participants	Objectives	Measurements	Conclusion about the relationship between exercise and eating disorders
		al measures	Scale Bulimia Test, The Family Environment Scale, Rosenberg Self-Esteem Scale, and Body Image Assessment	
Adkins and Keel (2005)	162 male and 103 female university students	to test whether the compulsive or excessive aspects of exercise are more closely related to eating disorders	Eating Disorder Inventory, Reasons for Exercise Inventory, and the Obligatory Exercise Questionnaire	Compulsive exercise may be a better definition than excessive exercise in connection with bulimia
Blumenthal, O'Toole, and Chang (1984)	compared 24 anorectics to 43 obligatory runners	to assess the similarity between Anorexia Nervosa and obligatory running	Minnesota Multiphasic Personality Inventory (MMPI); Clinical diagnosis based on the DSM II and the DSM III (Diagnostic and Statistical Manual of Mental Disorders)	Runners and anorectics are different. The relationship is superficial on the basis of the ten subscales of the MMPI.
Brewerton, Stellefson, Hibbs, Hodges, and Cochrane (1995)	110 anorexic, bulimic or both females grouped into compulsive and non-compulsive groups	to compare compulsively exercising and non-exercising patients suffering from eating disorders	Diagnostic Survey of the Eating Disorders; Clinical diagnosis based on the DSM III for Anorexia Nervosa and Bulimia Nervosa	Related compulsive exercise to elevated body dissatisfaction in patients with eating disorders and it was more prevalent (39%) in anorectics than in bulimics (23%).

Table 10.1. (Continued)

Author(s)	Participants	Objectives	Measurements	Conclusion about the relationship between exercise and eating disorders
Davis (1990a)	86 exercising and 72 non-exercising women	to compare body image and weight preoccupation between exercising and non-exercising women	Eysenck Personality Inventory; Body Image Questionnaire; and Subjective Body Shape; Eating Disorder Inventory (EDI)	Body-dissatisfaction was related to poorer emotional well-being in the exercise group only. EDI scores did not differ between the groups.
Davis (1990b)	53 exercising and 43 non-exercising women	to study addictiveness, weight preoccupation, and exercise patterns in a non-clinical population	Addictiveness with the Eysenck Personality Questionnaire (EPQ); Body Focus; Eating Disorder Inventory (EDI)	Addictiveness was related to weight and dieting variables in both groups and to perfectionism in the exercise group. EDI scores did not differ between the groups.
Davis, Brewer, and Ratusny (1993)	88 men and 97 women	to present a new "Commitment to Exercise" questionnaire and to study the relationship between exercising and obsessive compulsiveness, weight preoccupation and addictiveness	Addictiveness; Commitment to exercise; Obsessive compulsiveness; Eating Disorder Inventory (EDI), "Drive for Thinness" subscale	Presents validity and reliability data for the two factor (obligatory exercising and pathological exercising) "Commitment to Exercise Questionnaire. Excessive exercising was found to be distinct from eating disorders.
Davis et al. (1995)	46 anorexic patients, 76 high-level exercisers, 55 moderate exercisers,	to test the relationship between obsessive compulsiveness and	Commitment to exercise, Obsessive compulsiveness; Eating Disorder Inventory (EDI),	Weight preoccupation and excessive exercising were related in both high-level exercisers and anorectics.

Author(s)	Participants	Objectives	Measurements	Conclusion about the relationship between exercise and eating disorders
	all females	exercise in anorectics in contrast moderate and high-level exercising controls	"Drive for Thinness" subscale	
French, Perry, Leon, and Fulkerson (1995)	852 female students	to observe changes, over a three-year period, in psychological and health variables in dieting and non-dieting women	Negative emotionality; Self-concept; Eating Disorders Symptom Scores (based on DSM III), Restrained Eating Scale, Eating Disorder Inventory	Dieting habits were not related to physical activity levels over three years, but dieters reported greater decreases in physical activity than non-dieters.
French, Perry, Leon, and Fulkerson (1994)	1494 adolescents	to examine correlates of symptoms of eating disorders, including food preferences, eating patterns, and physical activity	Food preference and eating patterns questionnaires and Eating Disorders Symptoms	High-performance sport participation was found to be a predictor of eating disorders symptoms.
Levine, Marcus, and Moulton (1996)	77 females (44 assigned to regular walking and 33 controls) suffering from binge eating disorder	to examine the effects of an exercise intervention in the treatment of obese women with binge eating disorder	Beck Depression Inventory; Eating Disorder examination (a semi-structured clinical interview)	Binge eating disorder was successfully managed through a 24-week (aimed to burn 1000 calories per week) walking program

Table 10.1. (Continued)

Author(s)	Participants	Objectives	Measurements	Conclusion about the relationship between exercise and eating disorders
Mond, Hay, Rodgers, and Owen (2006)	3472 women who engaged in regular exercise	to better conceptuali ze the meaning of "excessive exercise"	A composite questionnaire measuring eating disorders, psychopathology, quality of life (health-related) psychological distress, and exercise behavior	Excessive is excessive when its postponement triggers guilt or when it is performed solely to influence weight or physical shape
Pasman and Thompson (1988)	90 participants (45 males and -45 females) equal in three groups: obligatory runners, obligatory weight lifters and sedentary controls	to examine body image and eating disturbance in obligatory runners and weight-lifters and in sedentary controls	Obligatory Exercise Questionnaire; Eating Disorders Inventory (EDI); Body Self relations Questionnaire (BSRQ)	Runners and weightlifters reported greater eating disturbance than controls. Females also reported greater eating disturbance than males.
Richert and Hummers (1986)	345 students	to examine the relationship between exercise pattern risk for eating disorders	Eating Attitude Test (EAT)	Exercise was positively correlated with EAT scores and participants with high EAT scores showed a preference for jogging.
Szymanski and Chrisler (1990)	66 female athletes and 20 non-athletes	to test the link between eating disorders, gender roles, and training	Bem Sex-Role Inventory; Eating Disorders Inventory (EDI)	Athletes scored higher on most subscales of the EDI than non-athletes.
Thiel, Gottfried, and Hesse (1993)	84 low-weight male athletes (25 wrestlers	to study the prevalence of eating disorders in	Eating Disorder Inventory (EDI)	52% of the athletes reported binging and 11% of the respondents evinced sub-clinical eating disorders.

Author(s)	Participants	Objectives	Measurements	Conclusion about the relationship between exercise and eating disorders
	and 59 rowers)	male athletes who, by the nature of their sport, are pressured to maintain low weight		Concludes that low-weight wrestles and rowers should be considered at risk for eating disorders.
Williamson et al. (1995)	98 female college athletes	to study the risk factors involved in the developme nt of eating disorders in female college athletes	Social Influence; Sports Competition Anxiety Test (SCAT); Athletic self-appraisal; Interview for Diagnosis of Eating Disorders	Validated a psychosocial model of risk factors for the development of eating disorders in female college athletes. the model suggests that social influence, performance anxiety and self-appraisal together influence body-size concern which in turn is a strong determinant of eating disorder symptoms
Wolf and Akamatsu (1994)	120 male and 168 female students classified as 159 exercisers and 129 non-exercisers	to study the relationship between exercise and eating disorders in college students	Eating Disorder Inventory (EDI); Eating Attitude Test (EAT)	Women involved in athletics demonstrated more anorectic/bulimic attitudes and greater weight preoccupation than non-exercising women but they did not manifest the same personality characteristics as female non-exercisers with the same level of eating disorder
Yates, Leehey, and Shisslak (1983)	60 male long-distance or trail runners	to study the similarity between obligatory running and Anorexia Nervosa	Interview	Found resemblance between obligatory running and Anorexia and, thus, marked the interest in further exploration of the relationship

The controversy between the above studies may be partly solved by considering the results of a study by Wolf and Akamatsu (1994) who studied female athletes who showed tendencies for eating disorders. These females, however, did not manifest the personality characteristics associated with eating disorders. Thus, in agreement with Blumenthal et al.'s (1984) and Knight et al.'s (1987) explanation, differences between obligatory exercisers and anorectic patients may outweigh substantially the similarities reported by Yates et al. (1983). In another theoretical article, Yates, Shisslak, Crago, and Allender (1994) also admit that the comparison of excessive exercisers with eating disordered patients is erroneous because the two populations are significantly different.

10.3. Prevalence of Eating Disorder Symptoms in Exercisers and Non-Exercisers

Davis (1990a; 1990b) and Davis, Brewer and Ratusny (1993) conducted a series of studies (Table 10.1) in which they examined exercising and non-exercising individuals and their tendency for eating disorders. In none of these studies was exercise behavior clearly related to eating disorders. Opposing these conclusions are the results reported by French, Perry, Leon, and Fulkerson (1994), Pasman and Thompson (1988), Richert and Hummers (1986), Szymanski and Chrisler (1990), and Wolf and Akamatsu (1994). Because similar measurements were used in general, the discrepancy between the two sets of studies may be most closely related to the definition of exercise. In the latter set of studies either excessive exercisers or athletes were tested in contrast to those tested in the first set. However, the definition of "excessive exercise" needs to be standardized in research. Four factors including mode, frequency, intensity, and duration, must be reported. Otherwise it is unclear what is meant by "excessive exercise" or "athlete". Reporting only one or two exercise parameter(s) is often insufficient, especially in studies dealing with eating disorders because the latter is suspected to occur only in a very limited segment of the physically active population.

The majority of the reviewed studies (10.1) suggest that a high level of exercise or athleticism is associated with symptoms of eating disorders. The determinants of this relationship are not well known. Williamson et al. (1995) proposed a psychosocial model for the development of eating disorder symptoms in female athletes (Figure 10.1). The authors revealed that overconcern with body size that was mediated by social influence for thinness, anxiety about athletic performance, and negative appraisal of athletic achievement, was a primary and strong determinant of the etiology of eating disorder symptoms. This model should be given serious consideration in the future and tested in several segments of the exercising population.

Although women are at higher risk for developing eating disorders (Yates et al., 1994), male athletes may be at risk too. For example, Thiel, Gottfried, and Hesse (1993) reported a high frequency of eating disorder symptoms and even sub-clinical incidences of eating disorders in low weight male wrestlers and rowers (Table 10.1). This report attracts attention to the fact that in some sports (i.e., gymnastics, boxing, wrestling), in which weight maintenance is critical, athletes may be at high risk for developing eating disorders. Athletes in these sports may turn to often "unhealthy", weight control methods (Enns, Drewnowski, and Grinker, 1987). This high-risk population, however, has received little attention in the literature. In the future more research should be aimed at this athletic population.

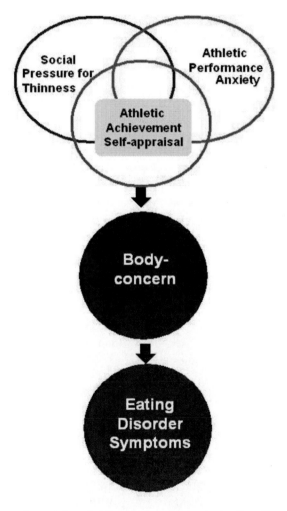

Figure 10.1. A psychosocial model for the development of eating disorder symptoms in female athletes proposed by Williamson et al. (1995).

The relationship between physical activity and eating disorders is not always negative. It is wrong to assume that exercise is directly related to eating disorders. Only a very small segment of the physically active population is affected negatively. One study, purposefully included in Table 10.1, has used physical activity successfully as a means of treatment for eating disorders. Levine, Marcus, and Moulton (1996) have shown that a simple walking regimen, performed three to five times a week and aimed to the burn 1000 calories, was efficient in managing binge eating disorders in a clinically diagnosed sample of obese women. In fact, about 71% of the experimental group was abstinent from binge eating by the end of the six-month study.

10.4. Is Excessive Physical Activity the Cause or the Consequence of Eating Disorders?

In view of De Coverley Veale's (1987) classification of "secondary exercise dependence" excessive exercise is a consequence of eating disorders. In these conditions exercise is used as a means for decreasing body weight (Blumenthal, Rose, and Chang, 1985; De Coverley Veale, 1987). However, Davis (1990a) argues that exercise may foster a higher degree of body narcissism and a distorted perception of one's body size which, in turn, may trigger eating disturbances. She suggests that it may be inappropriate to perceive exercise simply as the consequence of eating disorders. Indeed, some exercisers may resort to dieting for the sake of better performance (De Coverley Veale, 1987). However, to date there is insufficient evidence to claim that exercise may be a contributing factor to eating disorders. Therefore, the hypothesis proposed by Davis (1990a) needs further scrutiny. The model proposed by Williamson et al. (1995) may be a valuable starting point in future studies.

10.5. Recommendations for Future Research on Exercise Addiction and Eating Disorders

The majority of studies on the relationship between exercise and eating disorders have no conceptual foundation. Therefore, future studies need to use psychosocial models, such as that proposed by Williamson et al. (1995), to test the relationship and causality between physical activity and eating disorders. A clear definition of what is meant by *excessive exercise* or *high-level exercise* or *athlete* must be presented in future studies to allow for comparability with other studies. Currently some research is adding more confounding notions to this area of research. The conclusion of Mond et al. (2006) and their call for a new operational definition for excessive exercise as reference to quality rather than quantity (i.e. "exercise is excessive when its postponement is accompanied by intense guilt or when it is undertaken solely to influence weight or shape.") does certainly not help. By definition *excessive* refers to the *amount* or volume of exercise and if this characteristic is not as influential in eating disorders as some psychological constructs, like the nature and intensity of deprivation feelings when exercise is not possible or the motives for why exercise is undertaken, the correct operational definition should be adopted and standardized. Terms like *dysfunctional* exercise or *misused* exercise would surely be more adequate terms then *excessive* exercise. This is more than a problem with semantics. It is a shortage of operational definition without which no quality research could be carried out reliably. After resolving such basic problems, longitudinal studies that monitor both exercise behavior and eating habits, along with psychological factors such as anxiety, self-concept, body-image or body-concern, may be the most promising in the quest for a clearer understanding of the relationship between exercise and eating disorders.

Chapter 11

WHAT WE KNOW

- Exercise addiction is not the same as commitment to exercise.
- Exercise addiction is best understood in runners since other exercisers have received little attention in the literature.
- Exercise addiction is rare (approximately 3% of the exercising population is affected) but its consequences may be extremely severe.
- A significant proportion of people suffering from eating disorders resort to high levels of physical activity to lose weight. The condition is known as secondary exercise addiction or dependence.
- The personality characteristics of anorectics and highly committed exercisers are significantly different.
- A relationship between exercise and eating disorders is evident in athletic populations, particularly high-level exercisers and professional athletes.
- Female athletes, and those in sports participated in within weight categories, are at greater risk than other athletes of developing eating disorders.

Chapter 12

WHAT WE NEED TO KNOW

- What igniting events or factors trigger exercise addiction?
- What is the role of exercise history, anxiety, and self-esteem in the etiology of exercise addiction?
- To what extent is excessive exercising a consequence of eating disorders?
- Could moderate exercise have a positive effect on some eating disorders?
- What are the relationships between aspects of athleticism, body image/concern, exercise and eating disorders?
- What is the risk of competitive athletes developing eating disorders?

Chapter 13

CONCLUSIONS

13.0 - GENERAL CONCLUSIONS

Physical exercise in moderation seldom carries negative consequences. In most cases of psychological dysfunction associated with exercise behavior, physical activity is a means of coping with emotional problems. The coping mechanism could be abused, whether exercise, alcohol, or medication. The abuse of the former is rare because there is physical effort involved, in contrast to the latter two (Cockerill and Riddington, 1996). Thus genuine exercise addiction is relatively rare in the exercising population (Morris, 1989; Terry et al., 2004). People affected by eating disorders often use exercise as a means of weight control. Some correlates of excessive exercise are anxiety, low self-esteem, and long-term fidelity to the activity, as well as distorted body-image in some cases of eating disorders. Generally, excessive physical activity is unlikely to be a cause of psychological dysfunction, but rather a symptom of the latter.

APPENDIX A. THE EXERCISE ADDICTION INVENTORY

A. Terry, A. Szabo, and M. Griffiths

Directions:

Listed below are six statements about people's exercise habits. Using the scale below, please circle the number that reflects the degree to which you agree or disagree that the given statement applies to you.

1 – strongly disagree   2 – disagree   3 – neither agree nor disagree   4 – agree   5 – strongly agree

1) Exercise is the most important thing in my life

1	2	3	4	5

2) Conflicts have arisen between me and my family and/or my partner about the amount of exercise I do

1	2	3	4	5

3) I use exercise as a way of changing my mood

(e.g. to get a buzz, to escape etc.)   1   2   3   4   5

4) Over time I have increased the amount of exercise
I do in a day.   1   2   3   4   5

5) If I have to miss an exercise session I feel moody
and irritable   1   2   3   4   5

6) If I cut down the amount of exercise I do, and then
start again, I always end up exercising as often as
I did before   1   2   3   4   5

REFERENCES

Ackard, D. M., Brehm, B. J., and Steffen, J. J. (2002). Exercise and eating disorders in college-aged women: profiling excessive exercisers. *Eating Disorders, 10*, 31-47.

Adkins, C.E., and Keel, P.K. (2005). Does "excessive" or "compulsive" best describe exercise as a symptom of bulimia nervosa? *International journal of Eating Disorder, 38*, 24-29.

Aidman, E. and Woollard, S. (2003). The influence of self-reported exercise addiction on acute emotional and physiological responses to brief exercise deprivation. *Psychology of Sport and Exercise, 4(3),* 225-236.

Albrecht, U., Kirschner, N.E., and Grüsser, S.M. (2007). *Diagnostic instruments for behavioral addictions: an overview.* GMS Psycho-Social Medicine, 4:Doc11, Retrieved February 21, 2008 from: http://www.egms.de/pdf/journals/psm/2007-4/psm000043.pdf

American Psychiatric Association. (1995). *Diagnostic and Statistical Manual of Mental Disorders.* (4th ed.). Washington, DC: American Psychiatric Association.

Baker, T.B., Piper, M.E., McCarthy, D.E., Majeskie, M.R., and Fiore, M.C. (2004). Addiction motivation reformulated: an affective processing model of negative reinforcement. *Psychological Review, 111*, 33-51.

Beck, A. T., Ward, C. H., Mendelson, M., Mock, J., and Erbaugh, J. (1961). An inventory of measuring depression. *Archives of General Psychiatry, 4*, 561-571.

Berk, L.S., Tan, S.A., Fry, W.F., Napier, B.J., Lee, J.W., Hubbard, R.W., Lewis, J.E., and Eby, W.C. (1989). Neuroendocrine and stress hormone changes during mirthful laughter. *American Journal of Medicine and Science, 298(6)*, 390-396.

Biddle, S. and Mutrie, N. (1991). *Psychology of Physical Activity and Exercise: A Health-Related Perspective*. Springer Verlag London Ltd.

Blumenthal, J.A., O'Toole, L.C., and Chang, J.L. (1984). Is running an analogue of anorexia nervosa? *Journal of the American Medical Association (JAMA), 252*, 520-523.

Blumenthal, J.A., Rose, S., and Chang, J.L. (1985). Anorexia nervosa and exercise: Implications from recent findings. *Sports Medicine, 2*, 237-247.

Bouchard, C., Shephard, R.J., and Stephens, T. (Eds.) (1994). *Physical activity, fitness, and health*. Champaign, IL: Human Kinetics.

Bozarth, M.A. (1994) Physical dependence produced by central morphine infusions: an anatomical mapping study. *Neuroscience and Biobehavioral Reviews, 18*, 373-383

Brewerton, T.D., Stellefson, E.J., Hibbs, N., Hodges, E.L., and Cochrane, C.E. (1995). Comparison of eating disorder patients with and without compulsive exercisisng. *International Journal of Eating Disorders, 17*, 413-416.

Brown, R.I.F. (1993). Some contributions of the study of gambling to the study of other addictions. In W.R. Eadington and J.A. Cornelius (Eds*.), Gambling behavior and problem gambling* (pp. 241-272). Reno: University of Nevada Press.

Carmack, M.A., and Martens, R. (1979). Measuring commitment to running: A survey of runners' attitudes and mental states. *Journal of Sport Psychology, 1*, 25-42.

Chapman, C.L., and De Castro, J.M. (1990). Running addiction: Measurement and associated psychological characteristics. *The Journal of Sports Medicine and Physical Fitness, 30*, 283-290.

Cockerill, I.M., and Riddington, M.E. (1996). Exercise dependence and associated disorders: a review. *Counselling Psychology Quarterly, 9*, 119-129.

Coen, S. P., and Ogles, B. M. (1993). Psychological characteristics of the obligatory runner: A critical examination of the anorexia analogue hypothesis. *Journal of Sport and Exercise Psychology, 15*, 338-354.

Conboy, J.K. (1994). The effects of exercise withdrawal on mood states of runners. *Journal of Sport Behavior, 17*, 188-203.

Costa, P.T., Jr., and McCrae, R.R. (1992). *Revised NEO Personality Inventory and five-Factor Inventory Professional Manual*. Odessa, Fl: Psychological Assessment Resources.

Cousineau, D., Ferguson, R.J., De Champlain, J., Gauthier, P., Cote, P., and Bourassa M. (1977). Catecholamines in coronary sinus during exercise in man before and after training. *Journal of Applied Physiology, 43*, 801-806.

Crisp, A.H., Hsu, L.K.G., Harding, B., and Hartshorn, J. (1980). Clinical features of anorexia nervosa: A study of a consecutive series of 102 female patients. *Journal of Psychosomatic Research, 24*, 179-191.

Cumella, E.J. (2005). The heavy weight of exercise addiction. *Behavioral Health Management, 25(5)*, 26-31.

Dahlstrom, W. G., and Welch, G. S. (1960). *An MMPI Handbook*. Minneapolis, University of Minnesota Press.

Davis, C. (2000). Exercise abuse. *International Journal of Sport Psychology, 31*, 278-289.

Davis, C. (1990a). Body image and weight preoccupation: A comparison between exercising and non-exercising women. *Appetite, 15*, 13-21.

Davis, C. (1990b). Weight and diet preoccupation and addictiveness: The role of exercise. *Personality and Individual Differences, 11*, 823-827.

Davis, C., Brewer, H., and Ratusny, D. (1993). Behavioral frequencey and psychological commitment: Necessary concepts in the study of excessive exercising. *Journal of Behavioral Medicine, 16*, 611-628.

Davis, C., Kennedy, S.H., Ralevski, E., Dionne, M., Brewer, H., Neitzert, C., and Ratusny, D. (1995). Obsessive compulsiveness and physical activity in anorexia nervosa and high-level exercising. *Journal of Psychosomatic Research, 39*, 967-976.

De Coverley Veale, D.M.W. (1987). Exercise Dependence. *British Journal of Addiction, 82*, 735-740.

De Vries, H.A. (1981). Tranquilizer effect of exercise: A critical review. *The Physician and SportsMedicine, 9(11)*, 47-53.

Duncan, D.F. (1974). Drug abuse as a coping mechanism. *American Journal of Psychiatry, 131*, 724.

Eberle, S.G. (2004). Compulsive exercise: Too much of a good thing? *National Eating Disorders Association*. Retrieved October 23, 2007 from: http://www.uhs.berkeley.edu/edaw/CmpvExc.pdf

Edwards, P. (2007). Promoting physical activity and active living in urban environments. *Active Living, 16(5)*, 27-30.

Enns, M.P., Drewnowski, A., and Grinker, J.A. (1987). Body composition, body-size estimation and attitudes toward eating in male college athletes. *Psychosomatic Medicine, 49*, 56-64.

Estok, P.J., and Rudy, E.B. (1986). Physical, psychosocial, menstrual changes/risks and addiction in female marathon and nonmarathon runner. *Health Care for Women International, 7*, 187-202.

Evening Standard (2000). *Case history: Jackie's tale*. August 01, 2000. Retrieved February 21, 2008 from: http://www.thisislondon.co.uk/newsarticle-953584-details/Case+history%3A+Jackie%27s+tale/article.do

Eysenck, H. J., and Eysenck, S. B. G. (1991). *Manual of the Eysenck Personality Scale*. London: Hodder and Stoughton.

Farrell, P., Gates, W.K., Maksud, M.G., and Morgan, W.P. (1982). Increases in plasma b-endorphin/b-lipotropin immunoreactivity after treadmill running in humans. *Journal of Applied Physiology 52(5),* 1245-1249.

French, S.A., Perry, C.L., Leon, G.R., and Fulkerson, J.A. (1994). Food preferences, eating patterns, and physical activity among adolescents: Correlates of eating disorders symptoms. *Journal of Adolescent Health, 15*, 286-294.

French, S.A., Perry, C.L., Leon, G.R., and Fulkerson, J.A. (1995). Changes in psychological variables and health behaviors by dieting status over a three-year period in a cohort of adolescent females. *Journal of Adolescent Health, 16*, 438-447.

Frost, R. O., Marten, P., Lahart, C., and Rosenblate, R. (1990). The dimensions of perfectionism. *Cognitive Therapy and Research, 14*, 449-468

Furst, D.M., and Germone, K. (1993). Negative addiction in male and female runners and exercisers. *Perceptual and Motor Skills, 77*, 192-194.

Garner, D.M. (1991). *Eating Disorder inventory-2 manual*. Psychological Assessment Resources, Odessa, FL.

Garner, D. M., and Garfinkel, P. E. (1979). The eating attitudes test: An index of the symptoms of anorexia nervosa. *Psychological Medicine, 9*, 273-279.

Garner, D. M., Olmsted, M. P., and Polivy, J. (1983). Development and validation of a multidimensional Eating Disorder Inventory for anorexia and bulimia. *International Journal of Eating Disorders, 2 (2)*, 15-34.

Gibb, G. D., Bailey, J. R., Best, R. H., and Lambrinth, T. T. (1983). The measurement of obsessive-compulsive personality. *Educational and Psychological Measurement, 43*, 1233-1238.

Glasser, W. (1976). *Positive Addiction*. New York, NY: Harper and Row.

Godin, G. and Shephard, R.J. (1985). A simple method to assess exercise behavior in the community. *Canadian Journal of Applied Sport Science. 10*, 141-146.

Goldfarb, A.H. and Jamurtas, A.Z. (1997). b-Endorphin response to exercise: an update. *Sports Medicine 24(1),* 8-16.

Goodman, A. (1990). Addiction: definition and implications. *British Journal of Addiction, 85*, 1403-1408.

Griffiths, M.D. (1996). Behavioral addiction: an issue for everybody? *Journal of Workplace Learning, 8 (3)*, 19-25.

Griffiths, M. (1997). Exercise addiction: A case study. *Addiction Research, 5*, 161-168.

Griffiths, M.D. (2002). *Gambling and gaming addictions in adolescence.* Leicester: British Psychological Society/Blackwells.

Griffiths, M.D. (2005). A 'components' model of addiction within a biopsychosocial framework. *Journal of Substance Use, 10(4)*, 191-197.

Grüsser, S.M., and Thalemann, C.N. (2006). *Verhaltenssucht-Diagnostik, Therapie*, Forschung. Bern: Huber.

Hagan, A. L., and Hausenblas, H. A. (2003). The relationship between exercise dependence symptoms and perfectionism. *American Journal of Health Studies, 18*, 133- 137.

Hailey, B.J., and Bailey, L.A. (1982). Negative addiction in runners: A quantitative approach. *Journal of Sport Behavior, 5*, 150-153.

Hamer, M., and Karageorghis, C.I. (2007). Psychobiological mechanisms of exercise dependence. *Sports Medicine, 37(6),* 477-484.

Harte, J.L., Eifert, G.H., and Smith, R. (1995). The effects of running and meditation on beta-endorphin, corticotropin-releasing hormone and cortisol in plasma, and on mood. *Biological Psychology 40*, 251-265.

Haskell, W.L., Lee, I.M., Pate, R.R., Powell, K.E., Blair, S.N., Franklin, B.A., Macera, C.A., Heath, G.W., Thompson, P.D., and Bauman, A. (2007). Physical activity and public health: updated recommendation for adults from the American College of Sports Medicine and the American Heart Association. *Medicine and Science in Sports and Exercise, 39(8)*, 1423-1434.

Hausenblas, H.A., and Giacobbi, P.R. Jr. (2004). Relationship between exercise dependence symptoms and personality. *Personality and Individual Differences. 36*, 1265-1273.

Hausenblas H.A., and Symons Downs, D. (2002) Exercise dependence: a systematic review. *Psychology of Sport Exercise, 3,* 89-123.

Hausenblas, H.A., and Symons Downs, D. (2002). How much is too much? The development and validation of the exercise dependence scale. *Psychology and Health, 17*, 387-404.

Iannos, M., and Tiggemann, M. (1997). Personality of the excessive exerciser. *Personality and Individual Differences, 22*, 775-778.

Johnson, M.D. (1994). Disordered eating in active and athletic women. *Clinics in Sports Medicine, 13*, 355-369.

Johnson, R. (1995). Exercise dependence: When runners don't know when to quit. *Sports Medicine and Arthroscopy Review, 3*, 267-273.

Jones, R.D., and Weinhouse, S. (1979). Running as self-therapy. *Journal of Sports Medicine, 19*, 397-404.

Kjaer, M. and Dela, F. (1996). Endocrine Response to Exercise (pp. 6-8) In L. Hoffman-Goetz, (Ed.). *Exercise and Immune Function*. Boca Raton. CRC, 1.20, 1996.

Knight, P.O., Schocken, D.D., Powers, P.S., Feld, J., and Smith, J.T. (1987). Gender comparison in anorexia nervosa and obligate running. *Medicine and Science in Sports and Exercise, 19(suppl.)*, *396*, S66.

Lazare, A., Klerman, G. L., and Armour, D. J. (1966). Oral, obsessive and hysterical personalities patterns: An investigation of psychoanalytic concepts by means of factor analysis. *Archives of General Psychiatry, 14*, 624.

Levenson, H. (1981). Differentiating among internality, powerful others and chance. In H. Lefcourt (Ed.), *Research with the locus of control construct volume I: Assessment methods*. New York: Academic Press.

Levine, M.D., Marcus, M.D., and Moulton, P. (1996). Exercise in the treatment of binge eating disorder. *International Journal of Eating Disorders, 19*, 171-177.

Loumidis, K.S., and Wells, A. (1998). Assessment of beliefs in exercise dependence: the development and preliminary validation of the exercise beliefs questionnaire. *Personality of Individual Differences, 25*, 553-567.

Markoff, R.A., Ryan, P., andYoung, T. (1982). Endorphins and mood changes in long-distance running. *Medicine and Science in Sports and Exercise, 14*, 11-15.

McKinney, C.H., Tims, F.C., Kumar, A.M., and Kumar, M. (1997). The effect of selected classical music and spontaneous imagery on plasma β-endorphin. *Journal of Behavioral Medicine, 20(1)*, 85-99.

McLachlan, C.D., Hay, M., and Coleman, G.J. (1994). The effects of exercise on the oral consumption of morphine and methadone in rats. *Pharmacology, Biochemistry and Behavior 48(2)*, 63-568.

McNair, D. M., Lorr, M., and Droppelman, L. F. (1981). *Profile of Mood States Manual*. San Diego, CA: Educational and Industrial Testing Services.

Mond, J.M., Hay, P.J., Rodgers, B., and Owen, C. (2006). An update on the definition of "excessive exercise" in eating disorders research. *International Journal of Eating Disorders, 39*, 1047-153

Morgan, W.P. (1979). Negative addiction in runners. *The Physician and Sportmedicine 7*, 57-71.

Morgan, W.P. and O'Connor, P.J. (1988). Exercise and mental health. In R.K. Dishman (Ed.), *Exercise Adherence: Its Impact on Public Health*, (pp. 91-121). Champaign, IL. Human Kinetics.

Morris, M. (1989). Running round the clock. *Running, 104*, (Dec.) 44-45.

Pasman, L., and Thompson, J.K. (1988). Body image and eating disturbance in obligatory runners, obligatory weightlifters, and sedentary individuals. *International Journal of Eating Disorders, 7*, 759-777.

Péronnet, F., and Szabo, A. (1993). Sympathetic response to psychosocial stressors in humans: Linkage to physical exercise and training. In P. Seraganian (Ed.), *Exercise Psychology: The Influence of Physical Exercise On Psychological Processes* (pp. 172-217). New York: John Wiley and Sons.

Pierce, E.,, Eastman, N., Tripathi, H., Olson, K., Dewey, W. (1993). B- Endorphin response to endurance exercise: Relationship to exercise dependence. *Perceptual and Motor Skills. 77*, 767-770.

Pierce, E.F. (1994). Exercise dependence syndrome in runners. *Sports Medicine, 18*, 149-155.

Richert, A.J., and Hummers, J.A. (1986). Patterns of physical activity in college students at possible risk for eating disorder. *International Journal of Eating Disorders, 5*, 775-763.

Rosenberg, M. (1965). *Society and the adolescent self-image.* Princeton, NJ: Princeton University Press.

Rozin, P., and Stoess, C. (1993). Is there a general tendency to become addicted? *Addictive Behaviors, 18*, 81-87.

Rudy, E.B., and Estok, P.J. (1989). Measurement and significance of negative addiction in runners. *Western Journal of Nursing Research, 11*, 548-558.

Sachs. M.L. (1981) Running addiction. In M. Sacks and M. Sachs (Eds.), *Psychology of Running* (pp. 116-126), Champaign, ILL: Human Kinetics.

Sachs, M.L., and Pargman, D. (1979). Running addiction: A depth interview examination. *Journal of Sport Behavior, 2*, 143-155.

Sachs, M.L., and Pargman, D. (1984). Running addiction. In M.L. Sachs and G.W. Buffone (Eds.), *Running as therapy: An integrated approach* (pp. 231-252), Lincoln, NE: University of Nebraska Press.

Sforzo, G.A. (1988). Opioids and exercise: an update. *Sports Medicine 7*, 109-124.

Sforzo, G.A., Seeger, T.F., Pert, C.B., Pert, A., and Dotsen, C.O. (1986). In vivo opioid receptor occupation in the rat brain following exercise. *Medicine and Science in. Sports and Exercise, 18*, 380-384.

Smith, D., Hale, B., and Collins, D. (1998). Measurement of Exercise Dependence in Body Builders. *Journal of Sports Medicine and Physical Fitness, 38, 1-9.*

Speilberger, C. D., Gorsuch, R. L., Lushene, R., Vagg, P. R., and Jacobs, G. A. (1983). *Manual for the State-Trait Anxiety Inventory (STAI).* Palo Alto, CA: Consulting Psychologist Press.

Stoll, O. (1997). Endorphine, Laufsucht und Runner's High. Aufstieg und Niedergang eines Mythos. *Leipziger Sportwissenschaftliche Beiträge, 38*, 102-121.

Summers, J.J. and Hinton, E.R. (1986). Development of scales to measure participation in running. In Unestahl, L.E. (Ed.). *Contemporary Sport Psychology*, (pp. 73-84), Veje: Sweden.

Szabo, A. (1995). The impact of exercise deprivation on well-being of habitual exercisers. *The Australian Journal of Science and Medicine in Sport, 27*, 68-75.

Szabo, A. (2000). Physical activity as a source of psychological dysfunction. In Biddle S.J.H., Fox, K.R.,and Boutcher, S.H. (Eds.). *Physical activity and psychological well-being* (pp. 130-153). London: Routledge.

Szabo, A. (2006). Comparison of the psychological effects of exercise and humour. In Andrew M. Lane (Ed.). *Mood and Human Performance: Conceptual, Measurement, and Applied Issues* (Chapter 10, pp.201-216). Hauppauge, NY: Nova Science Publishers, Inc.

Szabo, A., Frenkl, R., and Caputo, A. (1996). Deprivation feelings, anxiety, and commitment to various forms of physical activity: A cross-sectional study on the Internet. *Psychologia, 39*, 223-230.

Szabo, A., Frenkl, R., and Caputo, A. (1997). Relationships between addiction to running, commitment to running, and deprivation from running. *European Yearbook of Sport Psychology, 1*, 130-147.

Szabo, A., Ainsworth, S.E., and Danks, P.K. (2005). Experimental comparison of the psychological benefits of aerobic exercise, humour, and music. *HUMOR: International Journal of Humor Research, 18(3)*, 235-246.

Szabo, A., and Griffiths, M.D. (2007). Exercise addiction in British sport science students. *International Journal of Mental Health and Addiction, 5(1)*, 25-28.

Szymanski, L.A., and Chrisler, J.C. (1990). Eating disorders, gender role, and athletic activity. *Psychology A Journal of Human Behavior, 27*, 20-29.

Tan, A. L., Kendis, R. J., Fine, J. T., and Porac, J. (1977). A short measure of eriksonian ego identity. *Journal of Personality Assessment, 41*, 279-284.

Taylor, D., Boyajian, J.G., James, N., Woods, D., Chicz-Demet, A., Wilson, A.F., and Sandman, C.A. (1994). Acidosis stimulates b-endorphin release during exercise. *Journal of Applied Physiology, 77(4)*, 1913-1918.

Terry, A., Szabo, A., and Griffiths, M.D. (2004). The exercise addiction inventory: A new brief screening tool. *Addiction Research and Theory, 12*, 489–499.

Thiel, A., Gottfried, H., and Hesse, F.W. (1993). Subclinical eating disorders in male athletes. *Acta Psychiatrica Scandinavica, 88*, 259-265.

Thaxton, L. (1982). Physiological and psychological effects of short-term exercise addiction on habitual runners. *Journal of Sport Psychology, 4*, 73-80.

Thompson, J.K., and Blanton, P. (1987). Energy conservation and exercise dependence: A sympathetic arousal hypothesis. *Medicine and Science in Sports and Exercise, 19*, 91-97.

Thompson, J.K., and Pasman, L. (1991). The obligatory exercise questionnaire. *Behavioral Assessment Review, May*, 116-118.

Thornton, E.W., and Scott, S.E. (1995). Motivation in the committed runner: Correlations between self-report scales and behavior. *Health Promotion International, 10*, 177-184.

U.S. Department of Health and Human Services – Public Health Service (2004). *Progress Review; Physical Activity and Fitness*. Retrieved 02 February 2008 from: http://www.healthypeople.gov/Data/2010prog/focus22/

Warburton, D.E.R., Nicol, C.W., and Bredin, S.S.D. (2006). Health benefits of physical activity: the evidence. *Canadian Medical Association Journal, 174(6)*, 801.809.

Wichmann, S., and Martin, D.R. (1992). Exercise excess. *The Physician and Sportsmedicine, 20*, 193-200.

Williamson, D.A., Netemeyer, R.G., Jackman, L.P., Anderson, D.A., Funsch, C.L., and Rabalais, J.Y. (1995). Structural equation modeling of risk factors for the development of eating disorder symptoms in female athletes. *International journal of eating Disorders, 17*, 387-393.

Wolf, E.M., and Akamatsu, T.J. (1994). Exercise involvement and eating disordered characteristics in college students. *Eating Disorders, 2*, 308-318.

Yates, A., Leehey, K., and Shisslak, C.M. (1983). Running-An analogue of anorexia ? *New England Journal of Medicine, 308*, 251-255.

Yates, A., Shisslak, C. M., Allender, J., Crago, M., and Leehey, K. (1992). Comparing obligatory to nonobligatory runners. *Psychosomatics, 33*, 180-189.

Yates, A., Shisslak, C.M., Crago, M., and Allender, J. (1994). Overcommitment to sport: Is there a relationship to the eating disorders? *Clinical Journal of Sport Medicine, 4*, 39-46.

INDEX

82

Index